Salt Lake City Underfoot

SELF-GUIDED TOURS OF HISTORIC NEIGHBORHOODS

Salt Lake City Under Foot

CENTENNIAL EDITION

SELF-GUIDED TOURS OF HISTORIC NEIGHBORHOODS

MARK ANGUS

Signature Books
Salt Lake City

To my mother,

Edna S. Angus,

for her continuous support.

I am indebted to many friends and colleagues who helped with this book. Martha Sonntag Bradley and Allen Roberts have given generously of their advice which I have relied upon heavily. Brent Corcoran spent many hours in historical research.

Linda Thatcher, Utah State Historical Society; Randall Dixon, LDS Church Historical Department; Mary Anne Greenwell-Plautz, Utah State Archives; and the staff at Special Collections, Marriott Library, provided leads to sources. The office of the County Surveyor provided aerial photographs from which Steve Parker produced the maps.

Thanks to Julie Easton and Connie Disney for their exterior and interior designs; to Ravell Call for his photographs; to Greg Jones for recording mileage on his bicycle odometer; to Boyd Payne for collecting information from parks, churches, and historic sites; and to the rest of the staff at Signature Books for their editing, proofing, and hours of walking to double-check for accuracy.

Cover Design by Julie Easton

97   96   6   5   4   3   2

Library of Congress Cataloging-in-Publication Data
Angus, Mark N.
Salt Lake City underfoot : self-guided tours of historic neighborhoods
/ Mark N. Angus. — Centennial ed.
    p. cm.
    Includes Bibliographical references and index.
    ISBN 1-56085-105-8 (Centennial Edition)
1. Walking—Utah—Salt Lake City—Guidebooks. 2. Bicycle touring—
Utah—Salt Lake City—Guidebooks 3. Salt Lake City (Utah)—
Guidebooks. I. Title.
GV199.42.U82S243   1996
917.92'258—dc20   96-6997
                                              CIP

Contents

Introduction

Great Salt Lake City was founded 24 July 1847 by Mormon pioneers led by Vermont carpenter Brigham Young. By 1869 more than 60,000 immigrants had reached Utah territory by covered wagon or handcart, and that same year the transcontinental railway linked the east and west coasts at Promontory, Utah, making immigration easier. In 1896 Utah became a U.S. state. Salt Lake City, its capital, derives its name from the largest inland lake west of the Mississippi River, with the second highest salt content of any body of water in the world.

This book offers views of several historic Salt Lake City neighborhoods, divided into round-trip tours. The intent is to provide an introduction to the city for visitors and, for locals, to complement histories and architectural studies already available.

The walking tours include some footpaths and byways not accessible by vehicle, although one can take a smorgasbord approach and check out what looks interesting by car. For those on foot, remember that our city blocks, laid out on a grid based on four cardinal compass points, are larger than usual. Should you have extra time, optional side trips are included in the text but not indicated on the accompanying maps. The bicycling tours follow designated city bicycling routes where they exist. To complete round-trip tours, some nondesignated routes are included, as well as some dirt trails. Please remember to wear a helmet and obey traffic signals and rules.

A few tips if you are on foot. You should not try walking if you are unaccustomed to a medium amount of daily exercise. Wear comfortable shoes. You may also want to take a small bottle of water or sports-drink. In summer it is advisable to wear a hat, sunglasses, and sunscreen. Although I have tried to avoid dangerous parts of town, I would not recommend carrying valuables or beginning a tour late in the evening.

A note about our street names. If you ask for directions and are told to go to "Second North," this means 200 North, the second street north of the city center. Similarly, "Twenty-first West" is 2100 West, twenty-one blocks west of the meridian. Locals view the city in terms of blocks from a central point and unconsciously abbreviate. If you are from the Northwest, where eastern streets run east and southern streets run south, keep in mind that in Salt Lake City "East" lies east (running north and south) and "South" lies south (running east and west). Should you become confused, remember that the mountains lie east of the city and streets labeled "East" run parallel to them.

Regarding Utah's liquor laws: First of all, don't try to order a drink before noon. You will be encouraged (or required) to order food with your drink, and you may not have more than one drink per person at your table. Not all restaurants are licensed to serve alcohol. Some serve only beer. Others serve wine but not mixed drinks. Some are allowed to add "flavorings" to drinks (liqueurs, etc.) but may not serve anything akin to a Long Island Iced Tea. Private clubs may serve almost anything in measured amounts, and most clubs offer temporary memberships for five dollars. If you can find a state liquor store, you can buy your own alcohol in whatever quantities, but you may not take it with you to a restaurant. Although state-run stores are few and far between, they are well-stocked, and a few downtown hotels have stores in their lobbies.

If you can comprehend the liquor laws and city streets, you are ready to begin exploring. If you are still confused, don't be deterred because locals are eager to help. If you are a visitor using this guide, you will be among the few who venture beyond tourist-oriented public relations sites to discover the rest of the city. I hope you find it rewarding.

A Brief History of Pioneer Utah

An important crossroads to California and Mexico, Utah has always been at the center of the "wild west." Such legends as Jim Bridger, Butch Cassidy, and Joe Hill, and recently such western folk heroes as Edward Abbey and Wallace Stegner have championed this mountain and desert terrain and their natural wonders.

The first permanent inhabitants of the Great Basin were the Anasazi cliff dwellers, known for their petroglyph rock art and advanced social order, who disappeared mysteriously in the fourteenth century. The later Utes, Paiutes, and Goshutes are related to the Shoshone of Idaho. Their first contact with Anglos was along the Old Spanish Trail where slave trade was conducted. Children of weaker bands were sold to Mexican dealers who auctioned them in Santa Fe and Los Angeles.

Fathers Escalante and Dominquez, Franciscan priests, are the first known Europeans to enter Utah, leaving Santa Fe in July 1776 to find a direct route to Monterey. Forty-eight years later, trappers Jim Bridger and Etienne Provost thought they had discovered part of the Pacific Ocean when they happened on the Great Salt Lake.

When Mormons arrived in 1847, following the trail of the Donner-Reed Party, they settled on the border between warring tribes and managed to befriend many of them, converting four tribal chiefs. But Mormons had their own agenda—to establish a new country outside the boundaries of the United States. Deseret, as they called it, was to include land now divided among Utah, Wyoming, Colorado, Nevada, and southern California. In an unexpected turn of events the following year, the Treaty of Guadalupe Hidalgo transferred "Upper California" from Mexico to the United States and Utah became a U.S. territory in 1850.

Mormon lobbyists in Washington, D.C., persuaded U.S. president Millard Fillmore to appoint Brigham Young as territorial governor and two of Young's followers as marshal and U.S. attorney. The territorial chief justice, associate justice, and secretary were to be eastern non-Mormons, which rankled Young. When associate justice Perry Brochus arrived in August 1851, he was greeted by Native Americans who relieved him of his clothing, obligating him to enter the city in his undershorts.

Young then ordered the marshall to confiscate the territorial seal, press, and money in the secretary's possession. Although federal officials were to oversee territorial elections, Young orchestrated a mock election two weeks after their arrival with only one candidate per office. The elections were declared illegal. Young defiantly convened the legislature in remote Fillmore, Utah, away from federal oversight, and the eastern officials resigned in protest.

The antagonism toward outsiders stemmed from the treatment Mormons received in Ohio, Missouri, and Illinois, where they had been driven from their homes. In Missouri, Governor Lilburn Boggs had issued the following proclamation in 1838: "Mormons must be treated as enemies, and must be exterminated or driven from the state if necessary for the public peace." An appeal to U.S. president Martin Van Buren had met with apology: "I can do nothing for you. If I do, I shall come in contact with the whole state of Missouri. Your cause is just, but I can do nothing for you."

When new federal officials were appointed to Utah territory in 1855, they were treated with renewed contempt. After crossing swords with Brigham Young, Judge Leonidas Shaver was found dead in his office (the local coroner said it was from an ear infection). The justices' offices were ransacked. Secretary Almon Babbitt, a lapsed Mormon, tried to leave the territory and was killed by "Indians," although Young's bodyguard Orrin Porter Rockwell was seen in the area prior to the incident. The justices' offices were again looted and their books and papers thrown into an outhouse and burned.

Brigham Young wrote to lobbyists, "Tell [U.S. president] Mr. Franklin Pierce that the people of the territory have a way—it may be a very peculiar way but an honest one—of sending their infernal, dirty, sneaking, rotten-hearted, pot-house politicians out of the territory and if he should come himself it would be all the same." Young wrote to the *Baltimore Sun*, "President Pierce and all hell could not remove me from office."

Meanwhile, Utah territorial chief justice William Drummond, who lived with a mistress, publicly moralized about the evils of polygamy and was run out of the territory. Back in Washington, D.C., in 1857, he reported conditions to newly instated U.S. president James Buchanan. Alarmed, Buchanan ordered 2,500 troops to the territory to remove Young from office and install a new governor. Young declared martial law and announced "that the thread was cut between us and the U.S. and no officer appointed by the government [will] come and rule over us from this time forth."

A standing army of 1,000 Mormon volunteers began establishing batteries in the canyons, diverting creeks across roads, and engaging in skirmishes with approaching troops. Salt Lake City was evacuated; local militia awaited Young's order to torch the city. As winter set in, federal troops languished in the mountains, while Mormon refugees huddled in makeshift shelters south of the valley. Faced with few alternatives, Young finally abdicated. The new governor, Alfred Cumming of Georgia, agreed not to station troops within the city, establishing Camp Floyd to the southwest.

Cumming served three years until the Civil War, then returned to his home state. His replacement, John Dawson, stayed three weeks, was beaten by vigilantes on his way out of the territory, and died soon thereafter. The next governor stayed one year and fled.

Abraham Lincoln's Republican Party, which opposed the "twin relics of barbarism": slavery and polygamy, guaranteed by their rhetoric Utah's sympathy with the secessionist South. Church leaders refused to furnish the Union with recruits, publicly hailed the dissolution of the United States, and predicted independence for Utah. Lincoln responded by establishing Fort Douglas at Salt Lake City. What followed was a war of words, political posturing, demonstrations of fire power, and legal feuds—but no Gettysburg.

At the close of the Civil War, Brigham Young began consolidating economic power, forbidding Mormons from doing business with "gentiles" and inviting outside merchants to leave. He was opposed by his own secretary, George Watt, and prominent Mormon merchant William Godbe. Others joined them in what was called the New Movement, including Mormon apostle Amasa Lyman, newspaper editor Edward Tullidge, historian Thomas Stenhouse, architect Elias Harrison, and freighter Henry Lawrence. Although these dissenters were excommunicated, they founded the influential *Mormon Tribune* which continues today as the *Salt Lake Tribune*.

In the 1880s the Republican-dominated U.S. Congress passed legislation outlawing polygamy. Mormon leaders were jailed and church property confiscated. In 1890 church president Wilford Woodruff capitulated on polygamy, although church leaders secretly performed plural marriages over the next twenty years. In an effort to gain statehood, Mormon leaders cajoled adherents into joining the Republican Party—which many reluctantly did—and greased the political machinery with over $1 million in "gifts" to politicians and journalists to see Utah, in 1896, become the forty-fifth state.

In the twentieth century Utahns have become assimilated into mainstream American culture. Ultra-patriotism, emphasis on nuclear-family values, and clean living typify Utah life today—perhaps as a reaction to the perceived stigma of grandparents' lifestyles. Although some Utahns preserve old ways (there are about 30,000 intermountain polygamists), Utah has become more cosmopolitan. Women and minorities are emerging in positions in business, science, government, and the arts. Preservation of historic buildings and the environment are becoming important social issues. Scientific discoveries include development of the first artificial heart. Utah's scenery has become a familiar backdrop in motion pictures, including the opening graphics for *Star Wars*.

This guide attempts to integrate tidbits from Utah's heritage into the current landscape. In the race to keep up with world trends, it is easy—and advantageous for some—to forget the past, ignoring a colorful heritage that, as you will see, is often more interesting than fiction.

WALKING TOURS

I.
Downtown Business District

DISTANCE: 3 MILES   TIME: 4 HOURS

Begin inside the center north gate (50 West North Temple Street) of the 10-acre walled city block which comprises the spiritual heart of the Church of Jesus Christ of Latter-day Saints (LDS), the Mormons. Parking is available north of Temple Square.

Information about LDS beliefs and practices is available in the North and South Visitors' Centers. The South Visitors' Center features presentations on LDS temples and the Book of Mormon. The North Visitors' Center, which stands on the site of the old LDS Endowment House (a temporary temple), houses an 11-foot marble replica of Danish sculptor Bertel Thorvaldsen's "The Christus," murals of Old and New Testament scenes, and multi-language video presentations. Forty-five-minute tours of Temple Square begin at the 100-foot flagpole every 5-10 minutes. Open 9:00 a.m.-9:00 p.m. (8:00 a.m.-10:00 p.m., summer); admission is free. Each year at Christmas time the block is festooned with some 300,000 colored lights.

The cathedral-like temple with lofty Gothic spires is the first structure to your left inside the center north gate. Admission is restricted to faithful Mormons. The interior includes marble floors, muraled walls and ceilings, Tiffany stained glass windows (some jeweled), hand-carved cherry-wood staircases, crystal chandeliers and mirrors, and gilded Beaux Arts ornamentation. The exterior is said to resemble the Masonic Temple in Philadelphia.

Look first at the crenelated battlement nave with alternating arched and round windows, then at the bas-relief details on the west side of the temple as seen from the flagpole.

1. Mormon Temple (50 West North Temple Street)

The quartzite for this stunning $4-million castellated (castle-like) Gothic Revival masterpiece was quarried in Little Cottonwood Canyon, 20 miles to the southeast, and transported to the temple site by ox team and later railroad. Each block weighs about 3 tons.

The temple has six triple-tiered towers with minaret-like turrets at each corner of each tier; the turrets on the lowest tier are framed by parapets which serve as air vents. The towers are capped by copper finials with a 12.5-foot gold-leafed (over copper) angel on the highest eastern tower at a height of 210 feet. The angel weighs 1,500 pounds and stands on a spherical capstone which contains copies of Mormon scripture.

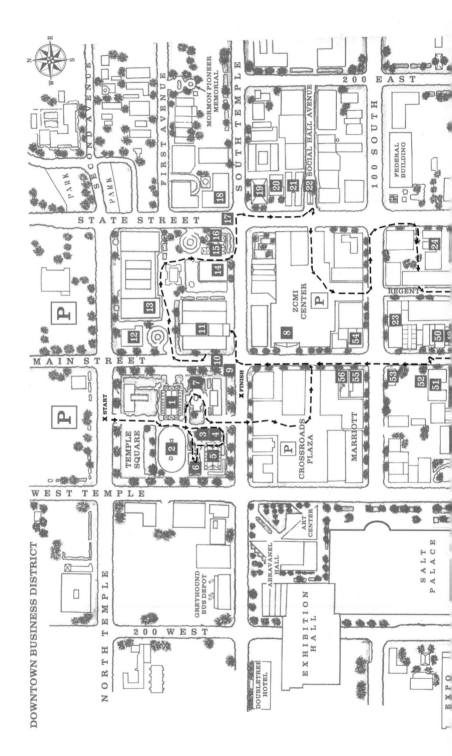

DOWNTOWN BUSINESS DISTRICT

The original temple plans called for gargoyles with faces of Mormon founders and walls built of adobe, which LDS church president Brigham Young believed would harden into rock. The architect, Truman Angell, persuaded Young to use quartzite instead. Angell, a carpenter, attended only two years of school as a child and had no formal training as an architect, making his accomplishment monumental.

It took forty years to build this magnificent temple, beginning in 1853, although construction was sporadic due to financial and political obstacles and design modifications. Work halted when drought required extra hands to help irrigate the valley settlement. Mormons filled in the original temple foundation to hide it from federal troops when the region was occupied during the Utah War of 1857. Work was stopped in 1868 when construction of the Union Pacific and Central Pacific rail lines diverted laborers, and again in the 1880s when church property was confiscated by the federal government. That a total of only fifteen years was spent in actual construction underscores the hardships associated with this enormous task.

On the west side of the temple, facing the domed tabernacle, are bas-relief suns, moons, stars—representing the three degrees of the Mormon heaven—and a Masonic-like handgrip of fellowship and Masonic all-seeing eye in the arches over the windows. Mormons enter the building from the north side through a subterranean tunnel from a small building known as the Temple Annex. Doors which open directly to the temple are sealed awaiting Jesus' second coming. The east doors were dynamited by vandals in 1962 but damaged only lightly.

The building to the west of the temple with the turtle-shell dome and sandstone buttresses is the Tabernacle.

2. LDS Tabernacle (Temple Square)

This oblong dome, designed by William Folsom and engineered by bridge builder Henry Grow, was completed in 1867. It provided the size and acoustical qualities necessary for large gatherings before the era of microphones. Although sound carried in the building, it also echoed until Truman Angell designed a horseshoe-shaped gallery to absorb sound waves. The unique "lattice-truss" roof resembles Grow's previous bridge designs. The roof surface was originally wood shingled, but in 1900 it was given a distinctive flat tin cover, which was replaced in 1947 by aluminum skin. In addition to iron nails, wooden pegs and rawhide thongs were used to hold the roof beams in place. Inside, pine benches and columns, finished to look like oak and marble, are original.

The organ is made of Utah pine. The grandeur of this imposing instrument is due in part to the visible gold-leaf pipes which are ornamental. The 11,613 functional pipes are hidden behind the façade. The organ was expanded to its current size in 1915. Originally the organ was powered by hand-pumped bellows, then reportedly by a City Creek water wheel. Two full-time technicians currently tune the organ daily. The building was completed and dedicated in 1875.

There are 30-minute organ recitals Monday-Saturday at noon, and Sunday at 2:00 p.m.; Mormon Tabernacle Choir rehearsal is Thursday, 8:00-9:30 p.m., and live broadcasts Sunday, 9:30-10:00 a.m. (audiences must be seated by 9:15 a.m.). Mormon Youth Symphony and Chorus rehearsals are Tuesday and Wednesday, respectively, 8:00 p.m. Admission is free.

Outside again, walk to the south side of the square to the granite pillar with gold-leafed bronze sea gulls on top.

3. Sea Gull Monument (Temple Square)

Utah's state bird is the California sea gull. Each spring for years after Mormon pioneers settled the valley in 1847 flocks of sea gulls devoured crickets which threatened crops. This was not seen as unusual at the time, but over the years the story of the sea gulls has taken on "miraculous" qualities. The commemorative monument was sculpted by Mahonri Young, grandson of Brigham Young, and erected in 1913.

South of the sea gull monument is the handcart monument.

4. Handcart Pioneer Monument (Temple Square)

In an incredible demonstration of devotion, 2,000 poor immigrants, impatient with delays, struck out across the Great Plains for Utah with nothing but a few personal possessions in hand-pulled carts. Brigham Young and other leaders resisted this influx of destitute refugees and worried about having to provide for them when they arrived. They were particularly concerned when two companies became bogged down in a winter storm in Wyoming in 1856 and had to be rescued. Young blamed subordinates for allowing the immigrants to leave their homes so late in the year. Today the handcart pioneers are eulogized for their faith, and it is a source of pride for Mormons to claim descent from handcart pioneers. The monument was sculpted by Torleif Knaphus in 1926.

Northwest of the handcart monument is the Carpenter's Gothic Assembly Hall.

5. LDS Assembly Hall (Temple Square)

This beautiful edifice dates from 1880 and sits on ground once occupied by a barn-like structure known as the Old Tabernacle and an open-air, thatched-roof bowery used during the summer. Notice the decorative woodwork—the frieze under the front gable and the flared fascia on the entrance pediment. The gabled cornices on the corner turrets have spear-and-pendant decoration. The building is topped by an elaborate wooden cupola. Four of the towers are blunt-topped and originally served as chimneys. The walls are quartzite. Notice the decorative glass windows and the Star of David in the rosette window, reflecting Mormon affinity with Old Testament Judaism and the belief that Mormons are descendants from biblical Ephraim. The hall was designed by Obed Taylor, a Mormon convert.

The interior, which is open to the public, includes a baroque pipe organ. The ceiling was originally muraled, but the art has been painted over. The Assembly Hall hosts the Temple Square concert series Friday and Saturday, 7:30-8:30 p.m. Admission is free but limited to those over the age of eight years.

Between the Assembly Hall and Tabernacle, against the west wall, is the Nauvoo Bell.

6. Nauvoo Bell (Temple Square)

This bronze bell, which rings hourly, was rescued from an Illinois Mormon temple dedicated in 1846 and later destroyed by fire. The bell is housed in a centennial campanile.

Rest rooms are located to the south of the bell, behind the Assembly Hall. North of the bell, just past the Tabernacle, is an entrance to underground tunnels where LDS security offices are located and church leaders are provided safe passage among downtown buildings.

From the bell, backtrack east and continue walking between the temple and South Visitors' Center, past the fountain on your left, to the statues of Mormonism's founding prophet and his older brother, the patriarch.

7. Joseph and Hyrum Smith Statues (Temple Square)

These memorials to Mormonism's founders, who were assassinated in Nauvoo, Illinois, were sculpted in 1907 by Mahonri Young and placed in the alcoves on either side of the ornate east temple doors. Young's other sculptures include "The Man With the Pick" in New York City's Metropolitan Museum of Art and "Joe Ganz" at Madison Square Gardens.

When you have finished visiting the temple grounds, exit through the center south gate. Horse-drawn carriages parked here provide city tours, and Old Salty, a train on wheels, offers a narrated tour beginning at 11:00 a.m., 1:00 p.m., and 3:00 p.m.

Across the street is Crossroads Plaza, a 4-level shopping mall which occupies nearly an entire city block. Rising above the mall is the 20-story Key Bank tower. Utah Woolen Mills, in the Temple View Center west of the mall, has been in business since 1905.

Cross South Temple Street south and enter the mall. Walk past the stairs and elevator to the escalator in the center of the mall. Turn left and proceed east, exiting onto Main Street, nicknamed Whiskey Street in the mid-nineteenth century when it was lined with saloons. Take a moment to glance across the street at the façade of the ZCMI department store.

8. ZCMI (50 South Main Street)

Zion's Cooperative Mercantile Institution (ZCMI) was created in 1868 by the LDS church to facilitate self-sufficiency, coupled with a boycott of non-Mormon merchants. Eventually there were 146 cooperative branches throughout the territory, making ZCMI the oldest quasi-

LDS Assembly Hall (I.5)

department store chain in the United States. Part of the 1876 cast iron façade has been retained.

Turn left and head north. To your left (west), the red sandstone Key Bank façade was partially salvaged from the 1869 Amussen Jewelry Company building which stood a little further south and was designed by Tabernacle architect William Folsom. The building had a balcony which was used as a bandstand for afternoon concerts. The second floor was the residence of Carl Amussen and his three wives. Of eighteen children, the youngest, Flora, became wife of former Mormon church president Ezra Taft Benson. Continue north to the corner of South Temple Street.

The southwest corner on which you are standing was the site of the Council House until it burned to the ground in mid-1883. The Council House housed the Mormon shadow government known as the Council of Fifty. It also served as LDS church administrative offices. Currently under construction at this site is the 17-20-story Gateway Building, owned by the LDS church.

Across the intersection on the southeast corner is the 18-story Kennecott Building, with Zion's First National Bank on the ground level. Built in 1960, this highrise sits on the site of frontier Mormon leader Ezra T. Benson's and mayor Daniel Wells's homesteads. The Kennecott building was built by the Mormon church. Although the copper company is a major tenant, the building never belonged to Kennecott.

Cross South Temple Street north. The meridian marker is a small stone shaft, enclosed within a protective railing, immediately on your left at the southeast corner of the temple wall.

9. Salt Lake City Meridian Marker (Main and South Temple Streets)

This marker defines the boundaries of Temple Square and serves as the originating point for the city's street numbering system, established by Orson Pratt in August 1847. The stone marker was later set by U.S. surveyor general David Burr. The Mormon city plan of wide streets and consistently numbered, uniform blocks was visionary. The numbering may be confusing at first, but, when oriented, maps are practically unnecessary and inner-city congestion typical of New England towns with narrow, winding alleys virtually non-existent.

Street names define how many blocks—east, west, north, south—they are from Temple Square. Main Street and South Temple Street are the 0 points. 700 East Street is seven blocks east of Temple Square. (Seven blocks equal one mile, or 1.6 km.) Addresses read as map coordinates. For example, 250 South 300 West is 2.5 blocks south of Temple Square on 300 West Street.

Behind the meridian marker, notice the sandstone base to the 13-foot high adobe wall surrounding the temple, preserved since 1857. Also on this same corner, notice the bust of Utah's famous pioneer photographer Charles Savage, remembered here as founder of Old Folks' Day.

Facing east, notice the Brigham Young monument in the center of Main Street just north of the crosswalk.

10. Brigham Young Monument (Main and South Temple Streets)

This statue by Springville, Utah, sculptor Cyrus Dallin features Brigham Young, early western explorer Peter Ogden, Shoshone chief Washakie, and a generic settler. The statue, commissioned by LDS church president Wilford Woodruff, was first displayed at the 1893 Chicago World's Fair and then stood on Temple Square until 1897. The names of those who accompanied Young into the valley in 1847 are listed on the north side of the monument. They include 140 free men, three women, two children, and three black slaves (here referred to as "colored servants"). One of them, Green Flake, drove Young's carriage into the valley and was later given to Young as tithing. Folklore to the contrary, Young was among the last of the vanguard party to see the valley. Because of a fever, he was left behind, and by the time he saw the valley, others were already planting potatoes.

Walk eastward across Main Street, passing the Brigham Young monument on your left. As you cross the street, listen for the audible traffic signals that assist the blind. "Cuckoo" means a green light for east-west travel; "chirps" a green light for north-south travel. These signals have been installed at ten downtown intersections.

At the northeast corner of South Temple and Main streets is the city's "grand dame hotel," the old Mormon-owned Hotel Utah, recently converted to office space and renamed the Joseph Smith Memorial Building. Renovation cost $42 million. Continue a few steps east to the porticoed main entrance facing South Temple Street and enter the building.

11. Hotel Utah (15 East South Temple Street)

This 10-story hotel was completed in 1911 for the Mormon church and some non-Mormon investors. It ceased operation in 1987 after shots were reportedly fired at the Church Administration Building from the hotel roof and issues of alcohol and patron behavior were raised by church authorities. Originally the hotel included a bar, which, though defended by church president Joseph F. Smith, proved to be a source of controversy. Until the 1950s blacks were excluded from the hotel; Harry Belafonte and Ella Fitzgerald are among those refused accommodations. Currently six of the ten floors are vacant.

One of the most colorful characters to haunt the hotel's past was Greek godfather (*padrone*) Leonidas Skliris, who lived and worked out of the hotel. Skliris exacted monthly fees from Greek workers and demanded loyalty to Greek establishments. When he provided mining companies with strike breakers from mainland Greece in a dispute involving Cretes, it resulted in the assassination of his assistant and Cretan loyalty to labor unions—signalling his demise. Other famous tenants included mining magnate Daniel Jackling and, in the 1930s, Utah governor Henry Blood.

Reflecting Italian Renaissance design, the building boasts a glazed enamel brick and terra-cotta façade over concrete. Terra-cotta lions' heads grace the decorative window framings. Construction of the hotel played an important role in the state's history of resistance to labor unions when dynamite bombs twice delayed work on the building.

Walking through the richly decorated lobby, notice the new marble floors, faux-marble columns, brass banisters, rococo plaster ceiling decoration, and original art-glass skylight. The statue of Joseph Smith is a copy of a Mahonri Young bronze. At the north end of the lobby are elevators to the 10th-floor Roof cafe (with retractable skylight) and Garden restaurant (no coffee or alcohol), as well as observation areas. The view of Temple Square is panoramic.

On the return elevator ride, you may want to stop at the mezzanine level to see the chapel (northeast corner) which preserves the ornate ceiling of what was formerly the Lafayette Ballroom. The Québecois organ and chandeliers are new but blend well with the frontier decor. The chapel serves three downtown LDS congregations. To return to the lobby, descend the broad staircase east of the elevators.

From the lobby, the hallway east of the staircase leads to the north end of the building and a wide-screen theater. The movie *Legacy* is based loosely on the diary and experiences of a frontier woman, Mary Elizabeth Rollins Lightner, a polygamous wife of Joseph Smith (though this fact is glossed over in the film). Monday-Saturday, 9:00 a.m.-8:30 p.m., 53 minutes, shows continuously, free.

Near the theaters is the Family Search Center. If you have 30 minutes, a staff of 200 volunteers at 130 computer workstations will help you construct your "pedigree" or family tree through the world's largest genealogical data base and provide you with a printout. Mormons practice posthumous, vicarious baptism and ritually "seal" family chains in temples. You can determine, from the computers, when your ancestors were baptized and sealed.

Return to the lobby elevators and exit to the west. You will pass the Empire Room on your right just before exiting. The murals depicting English hunting scenes are recent reproductions by Judith Mehr. Notice the beautiful woodwork and gilding. National Register of Historic Places.

When you emerge onto Main Street, turn right (north). The hotel occupies the original location of the tithing office and Deseret Store (and tithing barn), which served as a moneyless bank, post office, and internal revenue service for the first settlers. Loans, savings, payments, and receipts were transacted in grain, livestock, labor, and tithing scrip. Mormon church-owned *Deseret News*, the region's first newspaper, was located on the second story of the Deseret Store. "Deseret" was thought by Mormon founder Joseph Smith to mean "honeybee" in Hebrew. An enormous brick and plaster beehive cupola tops the Hotel Utah.

Continue northward. There is a walkway just before the underground parking entrance. Turn right and walk east through the plaza and grounds.

As you enter the plaza, to your immediate left over the parking entrance is the Relief Society Building.

12. Relief Society Building (76 North Main Street)

Founded in the early 1840s in Nauvoo, Illinois, the Relief Society is the women's auxiliary of the LDS church's all-male lay priesthood. Throughout the mid- to late-nineteenth century, Relief Society leaders exercised considerable independence in administering the society's benevolent programs and organizations. With the LDS church's emphasis on male priesthood during the twentieth century, the Relief Society has surrendered much of its autonomy. During the 1970s the Relief Society proved an effective lobby in helping defeat the Equal Rights Amendment. The building, which was completed in 1956, is composed of cast stone with red granite spandrels and decorative wheat sheaves.

Continue east along the walkway through the plaza. The next building you will encounter on your left (north) is the LDS Church Office Building.

13. Church Office Building (50 East North Temple Street)

This 28-story highrise, the city's tallest building, was originally designed to be 42 stories. It was constructed in 1972 for $38 million opposite the old Heber Kimball estate. The plain verticality of the architecture makes the building appear less imposing than it might otherwise be. Despite its height, it is not generally the first building people notice when they first see the city's skyline. Notice the illusion of lightness—the tall shaft hovering above two oval reliefs of the world at either side of the base. The style is influenced by French architect Le Corbusier's New Formalism. Tours begin in the main lobby and on the 26th-floor observation deck, 9:00 a.m.-4:30 p.m., Monday through Friday (also Saturdays, April through September). The church's history library and archives are housed in the east wing.

Turn right (south) opposite the Church Office Building entrance and begin traversing the alley between the 3-story Lion House on the left and 4-story granite-faced Church Administration Building on the right (directly south of the fountain).

14. Church Administration Building (47 East South Temple Street)

This building, completed in 1917 at a cost of more than $1 million, houses the presiding officers of the Mormon church and their staffs. It sits near the site of Brigham Young's earliest adobe home.

Considering that it was erected during World War I, it is an extravagant example of Neo-Classical Revival architecture, with twenty-four Greek Ionic columns weighing eight tons each. The building is constructed of steel and concrete faced with Utah granite. The interior is adorned with walnut, marble, onyx, and oriental rugs. Admission is restricted to church officers and their guests.

Only one woman has been officed in this building. She was Susa Young Gates, Brigham Young's daughter, sometimes referred to as the "thirteenth apostle." She married Alma Dunford, a dentist, divorced him, and married Jacob Gates. During the 1910-20's she was on the Relief Society general board, founded the *Relief Society Magazine* and the *Young Woman's Journal*, and was a delegate to the International Council of Women in London and Copenhagen.

As you continue south along the east side of the building, notice the lions' heads in relief on the cornice. On your left, in the Lion House, is the Pantry restaurant, open 11:00 a.m.-2:00 p.m. and weekends 5:30 p.m-9:00 p.m. (no coffee or alcohol).

15. Lion House (63 East South Temple Street)

Completed in 1856 for Brigham Young's families, this 2.5-story Gothic Revival adobe structure takes its name from the couchant lion on top of the front porch (sculpted by William Ward) and Young's nickname "Lion of the Lord." Note the shuttered windows, tall chimneys, and tile roof; east and west exposures are topped with ten steep-roofed gables.

Young, who had over fifty wives, intended the house as an example of the way such marital arrangements could be managed. The main floor contained bedrooms and parlors for twelve wives and young children, the second floor bedrooms for childless wives, the upper floor twenty children's bedrooms. A spacious, enclosed west porch served as a recreation area. A dining room seated seventy people. A large laundry room with an open fire and cauldrons operated twenty-four hours a day. Notice the rough-faced stone foundation. Young died here 29 August 1877. Public entrance is allowed to the restaurant and occasional receptions. No tours. National Register of Historic Places.

Continue east along South Temple to the Beehive House. Both the Lion and Beehive houses were designed by Brigham Young's brother-in-law Truman Angell.

16. Beehive House (67 East South Temple Street)

Completed in 1854 of adobe block, this attractive Greek Revival home was Brigham Young's official residence where he lived with his second wife Mary Ann Angell and later with Lucy Decker. The west wing of the house served as a reception center and office, and a north wing was added in the 1890s. The house also served as the residence of four subsequent church presidents and was the site of President Joseph F. Smith's vision of the afterlife just before his death in 1918. From the 1920s to the 1950s the house served as Young Women's Mutual Improvement Association quarters for young working women.

Atop the cupola is a beehive-shaped ornament. Notice the widow's walk and 2-story veranda—a southern-colonial accommodation to

Utah's long, dry summers. Inside, the pine woodwork has been stained to look like hardwood and marble. Half-hour guided tours are available daily, 9:30 a.m.-4:30 p.m. (10:30 a.m.-1:00 p.m Sundays). National Register of Historic Places.

Head east to the corner.

17. Eagle Gate (State and South Temple Streets)

This imposing arch straddling the street is an enlargement of one erected in 1859 to mark the entrance to City Creek Canyon Road, which ran across Brigham Young's compound to the canyon east of the state capitol. The original wooden eagle stood on a carved beehive anchored to a cobblestone wall surrounding Young's property. The larger bronze eagle, dating from 1963, weighs two tons and has a wing span of twenty feet.

Young's 8-foot-tall wall surrounding his 50-acre compound extended to the east side of the canyon. City Creek, which now flows underneath North Temple Street, blocked access to the canyon from the west. Young charged a toll for crossing his property to reach the canyon. The original wooden gate was secured by a Chinese puzzle-like lock. Young's compound included stables and a blacksmith shop.

Cross State Street to the east.

18. Eagle Gate Apartments (109 East South Temple Street)

Originally the site of Brigham Young's adobe schoolhouse, this corner was later developed by renowned "Silver Queen" Susanna Bransford. Her Bransford Apartments, which cost $150,000 to build, included an elegant dining room, live-in cooks, and servants' quarters above every apartment. Bransford inherited her first husband Albion Emery's mining fortune and went on to marry Chicago millionaire Edwin Holmes, Serbian doctor Radovan Delitch, and Russian prince Nicholas Engalitcheff. Her apartments were demolished in 1984 and the current structure erected in the 1980s, based loosely on the original design.

☛ Side Trip: For a side trip to Brigham Young's burial site, head north on State Street one-half block and turn right after the Gateway Apartments onto First Avenue (50 North). If you look closely, you may be able to catch a glimpse of the remaining section of cobblestone wall from the Young compound across the street to your left beginning at the end of the parking lot and continuing north into the Brigham Young Historic Park. The stone wall at the entrance to the park was built in 1995. Continue east, climbing the gradual incline three-fourths of a block to the wrought-iron enclosure on the right across the street from Castle Heights Apartments.

Beehive House (I.16)

The cemetery address is about 140 East First Avenue and bears a plaque reading "Mormon Pioneer Memorial." The graves are in the back, Young's in the southeast corner. Also buried here are several of Young's wives, including poet and lyricist Eliza Snow, Mary Ann Angell, and Lucy Decker.

To resume the tour, exit the cemetery, turn left, and retrace your steps back to State and South Temple streets. End Side Trip.

———

Cross South Temple Street to the south to the limestone bastian housing the Alta Club.

19. Alta Club (100 East South Temple Street)

Until recently a males-only club, this exclusive establishment was founded in 1883 by prominent non-Mormon businessmen (Mormons were excluded), primarily mining entrepreneurs, and named after the Alta mining district. It advertised "the comforts and luxuries of a home, together with the attraction of meeting each other in a pleasant and social way," which included availing one's self of a bar and high-stakes poker games. For a time the club housed slot machines.

Italian renaissance was the style used for American men's clubs in the late nineteenth century, identified by the horizontal differentiation into distinct stories, with arched doorways and windows and a molded belt course between floors. Notice especially the rusticated ground floor. The Alta clubhouse was designed by Cornell-educated Frederick Albert Hale and completed in 1897. Twelve years later the east wing was added, almost doubling the size and relocating the entrance from State Street to South Temple Street. The interior includes high ornate ceilings, crystal chandeliers, oak fireplaces, stained glass windows, and marble sinks. The west doors, bearing the "Guest Entrance" plaque, were the "ladies' entrance" after renovation and led directly to the second-story dining room. The site was acquired from a daughter of Brigham Young. Access is restricted to members and their guests.

Proceed south on State Street. Across the street to your right, notice the 22-story Eagle Gate Tower which stands on the site of the long-since demolished Gardo House, built for Brigham Young in Second Empire style but not completed until after his death. It was popularly called Amelia's Palace after Young's twenty-fifth wife Amelia Folsom. It was mostly used for entertaining. Susanna Bransford later lived there.

To your left, just past the Alta Club, is the old public library.

20. Salt Lake City Public Library (15 South State Street)

Despite its rather modest size in relation to neighboring structures, this building's Beaux Arts extravagance and oolite limestone create a visual image that attracts attention. Among the exuberant decorative details, notice the ornate keystones over the columns and the Flemish curve to the dormer façade. Now home to Hansen Planetarium and Space Science Library and Museum, this 1905 structure acquired the territory's 1,000-volume library funded by the U.S. Congress. The city library was open one day per week. Today science, star, and laser shows are presented mornings, afternoons, and evenings in a domed theater. National Register of Historic Places.

Continue south.

21. Belvedere Apartments (29 South State Street)

This is the site of Clara Decker Young's home—one of Brigham Young's wives. The LDS church built this 9-story, U-shaped apartment-hotel in 1919 and later traded it for land. It was advertised as the city's first "ultramodern" fireproof hotel. Be sure to notice the yellow and pink terra-cotta vases on the wall above the windows at street level.

Continue south to the glass-framed enclosure behind the historical marker.

22. Social Hall (39 South State Street)

Beneath this enclosure are the stone foundation walls of the first theater west of the Missouri River. Built in 1852, this Greek Revival playhouse seated 350. Tickets were purchased with gold dust, tithing scrip, and produce. The hall was rented by the Polysophical Society, founded by Lorenzo Snow (who later became LDS church president), which disbanded in 1856 when church leader Jedediah Grant called their intellectualism "a stink in my nostrils." City dances were held here, and the entrance fees included a discount for additional wives. This was the site of the Christmas riot of 1854, when locals clashed with U.S. soldiers sent to investigate the murder of a government surveyor.

The hall later housed the Latter-day Saint College, which evolved into the LDS Business College now located on South Temple Street. The hall was razed in 1922 as part of a $1-million commercial project featuring twenty-five automobile garages, showrooms, and workshops.

Entering the glass frame, which is the size and shape of the original structure, you can see Social Hall Avenue, which was lined with car dealerships through the 1950s. Descend the escalator to the basement-level historical exhibit and exit west through the underground tunnel into the ZCMI Center (closed Sundays). Walk through the mall atrium to the information desk. You may want to visit the shops and food court on the upper level and the 125-year-old Mormon bookstore, Deseret Book. Otherwise turn left and walk past the elevators and escalators to exit the mall through the south entrance.

Outside the mall, notice the narrow, red sandstone building across the street to the right, west of the new 5-story *Deseret News* building (under construction).

Salt Lake City Public Library (I.20)

23. Utah Commercial and Savings Bank (22 East 100 South Street)

Designed by Richard Kletting and constructed in 1890 for Francis Armstrong, Salt Lake City mayor and bank founder, this edifice is one of the best and few remaining examples of Richardsonian Romanesque architecture in the city. Massive, columned, and arched, the red sandstone is designed to look old and weathered and resemble 14th-century styling. As was common for commercial buildings, the sandstone façade hides a simpler brick structure. National Register of Historic Places.

Turn left and proceed east on 100 South Street to the corner of State Street. Here is where the Salt Lake Theatre stood until it was demolished in 1929 to make way for a gas station, preceding the current Art Deco telephone headquarters which was built in the 1940s. A corner plaque, facing State Street, commemorates the old theater.

Truman Angell's protégé William Folsom designed the stately theater. Folsom, like Angell, had no formal architectural training and, like Angell, was related to Brigham Young (father-in-law). The theater was built in 1862, one year before Folsom helped design the Tabernacle, using the Drury Lane Theatre in London as a model. As with the Tabernacle, the bell-shaped interior created an echo which had to be corrected—in this case with a flat ceiling. Like Social Hall, entrance fees were paid in grain, eggs, and even needlework. A front-row-center rocking chair was reserved for Brigham Young.

Turn right, crossing 100 South Street to the south. Notice across the street to your left (southeast corner) the 8-story Wallace Bennett Federal Building, an example of New Formalism. This is where the 1866 City Hall stood which was moved stone by stone to Capitol Hill and renamed Council Hall (not to be confused with Council House). To your right is the Salt Lake City branch of the Federal Reserve Bank of San Francisco.

Continue south one-half block to Orpheum Avenue and the theater after which it was named.

24. Orpheum Theatre (132 South State Street)

Built in 1905 as the city's first quality vaudeville theater, this is an example of Second Renaissance Revival Style with a 12-foot statue of Venus on top and relief male and female heads over the entrance. The playful façade was designed by architect Carl Neuhausen who also designed the Thomas Kearns mansion, the Cathedral of the Madeleine, and the Oregon Shortline Railroad building. The interior was equally festive and boasted green walls with gold trim, and draperies, seats, and carpeting in deep red with gold arabesque designs. In 1972 the LDS church restored this theater as the 1,100-seat Promised Valley Playhouse for semi-professional and amateur drama. This is also home to the Utah Opera Vocal School.

Standing in front of the theater, looking across State Street a bit to the south, you may be able to see an old brick harness shop—since covered with green aluminum siding—at 147 South State Street, built in 1889. Since 1949 the building has housed Radio City Lounge, reportedly the oldest gay bar west of the Mississippi River.

Proceed west on Orpheum Avenue under the parking terrace, passing Plum Alley to your left, once the heart of Chinatown, with cafes, shops, laundries, gambling halls, and two opium dens. At the end of Orpheum Avenue, turn left and proceed south on Regent Street, formerly the city's red-light district, originally—and appropriately—called Commercial Street. At the southern end of Regent Street is a red brick building on your left with a flat roof and pressed metal cornice. Now named the Felt Electric building, this was originally the Holmes establishment.

25. Holmes Brothel (165 South Regent Street)

This building is one of the city's few surviving nineteenth-century bordellos. A late-comer on the block, it was built in 1893 and operated as a brothel until about 1920. The building was owned by Gustave Holmes, director of the National Bank of the Republic and one of the wealthiest men in the city. Stephen Hays, Holmes's successor as bank director, owned a brothel next door at 169 Commercial Street. Although most houses of ill-repute were contained within this area, National Bank of the Republic founder Lewis Karrick owned a similar establishment on Main Street. A Commercial Street saloon and bordello were owned by city councilman Martin Mulvey, who also owned a saloon on State Street and a cigar and liquor store on Main Street. In 1908 there were thirty-five brothels and 150 prostitutes in this area of town. Women-for-hire paid the city a 10-dollar monthly registration fee.

Cora Thompson, of Svea's Rooming House, was one of the street's most famous madames. Others included Helen Blazes, who was financed by Utah Copper Company leader Daniel Jackling; Kate Flint, an intimate of U.S. senator Frank Cannon (Mormon apostle George Q. Cannon's son); and Ada Wilson who ran the "Palace" at 33 Commercial Street. In 1938 Mayor E. B. Erwin and chief of police Harry Finch spent eight months in jail for receiving payoffs from sixteen brothels, signalling the beginning of the end for institutionalized *amour*.

Continue south to 200 South Street. This is the site of a 1913 street battle between union Wobblies and Utah Copper Company thugs, when International Workers of the World activist James Morgan was pulled from his speaker's platform and beaten and six men hospitalized for gunshot wounds. This was the only street corner in town where the city would issue a permit for union activists to preach.

Proceed south at the crosswalk to the J. W. Gallivan Plaza. West of the plaza is the 24-story, Neo-Classical One Utah Center. Entering the plaza, notice the 15-ton sandstone, copper, and glass sundial by artist Kazuo Matsubayashi, called "Asteroid Landed Softly." Left of the sundial is a reflecting pool/skating rink and outdoor cafe.

Continue south across a small bridge to the plaza fountain that sprays downward from a green metal arch. Turn left and walk through the Activity Building which includes public restrooms. Exiting east, walk past the bird cage east across another bridge to State Street.

At State Street, notice the building across the street just a bit to the right (245 South State Street) with the blue trim. This was Nellie Olbrich's 1905 Chadbourne Hotel, now an art supply store and tenement hotel. Two buildings south was the 1909 Rex Burlesque Theater (255 South State Street), now Tivoli Gallery, Utah's largest private art gallery.

Turn right and proceed south on State Street to the corner. The gap in pre-twentieth-century structures along this block is due to the fact that Mormons built uptown and non-Mormons developed several blocks to the south. It took years for the two poles to merge. A number of historic buildings have been demolished.

At the corner of 300 South State Street is the magnificent Brooks Arcade.

26. Brooks Arcade (268 South State Street)

Already by 1891 German immigrant Julius Brooks, reportedly the first Jewish merchant to settle in Utah, was leasing space in this 3-story retail block built in rusticated Richardsonian Romanesque style. Notice the interesting variation in brick treatment, the round arches, broad pilasters, and weathered stone. The cornice also has interesting detailing. Brooks's arcade housed a variety of small shops—an early version of today's shopping center. Oculists, violin teachers, dentists, and printers all had offices here—and a hat and bagel shop was operated by Brooks's wife Fanny. In 1913 Herbert Auerbach bought the arcade for the Auerbach Department Store. Among other things, Auerbach's store cleaned ostrich-feather boas for $1.75. Although the building structure is brick, the two walls facing State Street and 300 South Street are veneered with gray-brown sandstone. Intended to be six stories tall, when settling was encountered at the third story, architects Dallas and Hedges recommended a modification. National Register of Historic Places.

Before continuing south, notice the glass and steel Broadway Centre highrise across the street to the left (northeast corner). Long before any construction was begun in the city, this corner was where the advance pioneer company planted their first crops—potatoes mostly—after a branch of City Creek was dammed to flood a wide field in preparation for plowing. City Creek was later channeled into canals to provide permanent irrigation. 300 South Street (Broadway) was originally called Emigration Road. Wagon trains lumbered along this trail to the old fort (300-400 West) then north to Union Square (200-300 North) for disembarkment. Union Square later became the University of Deseret campus and is now the site of West High School.

Cross 300 South Street to the south and walk to Exchange Place alley mid-block (355 South).

From here you can see the pastel green and pink Beaux Arts details on the commercial structure to the south (the corner of State Street and 400 South). This was the Federation of Labor Hall. Part of the "Hotel Plandome—European" advertisement on the building's north brick wall is also still visible. From here you can also see the Gallic towers of the City and County Building across the street to the southeast, topped by the statue of Columbia, with candle-snuffer domes, dormered gables, and fairy-castle balconies.

If you have time, walk to the corner to see the renovated labor hall and diagonally across the street to scrutinize the Romanesque masonry of the City and County building, especially the relief faces of prominent early Utahns and mythological characters. Then return to Exchange Place alley.

27. Salt Lake City Federation of Labor Hall (69 East 400 South Street)

Constructed in 1903, this hall was the scene of many union rallies and after-hours hell-raisers. It served twenty-five local unions affiliated with the American Federation of Labor. The AFL endorsed Socialist Party candidates in 1911, and the local membership pulled enough weight to elect Henry Lawrence, a socialist, to the county commission that year.

When the building was remodeled as Hotel Plandome in 1913, the "European" attraction was low-cost rooms with shared bathrooms. It now houses a restaurant on the ground floor and offices upstairs. Notice the metal mountain lions under the eaves and the marbleized iron pillar at the corner. Together with the molded cornice and variegated brick, the building is quite colorful.

28. City and County Building (451 South State Street)

Originally called the Unihalle, this imposing gray sandstone monument was erected in the early 1890s at a cost of $1.1 million for city and county offices. It was also, in effect, Utah's first state capitol. The Salt Lake City firm of Monheim, Bird & Proudfoot designed the intricate Romanesque details. The grounds, now known as Washington Square, are where the lead party of Mormon immigrants are thought to have camped upon entering the valley in late July 1847. For years thereafter this block served as a hay market and round-up point for cattle drives.

The faces and figures of men and women important to Utah's history can be found in the exterior stone work, as well as Masonic symbols of brotherhood, sacrifice, and eternity. Nearly 300 trees of forty-five varieties enhance the 10-acre grounds. The building was extensively renovated and placed on base-isolation springs to resist earthquake damage in the 1980s and today houses city government offices. Free tours of the beautiful interior are given on Tuesdays and Thursdays, or you can explore the heart of the building on your own. National Register of Historic Places.

Proceed west on Exchange Place alley to the historic buildings erected at the turn of the century as anchors for the city's non-Mormon business section. Equally important for its sense of space as its architecture, Exchange Place creates the sense of a place apart through its inward-facing buildings. Notice the warm brick colors which help create an inviting urban environment. Exchange Place is on the National Register as a historic district. Past the multi-level parking garage (where, from the roof, you can get a closer look at the colorful cornice levels of these buildings, if you would like to), to your right, fronted by four 2-story columns, is the old stock exchange.

29. Salt Lake Stock and Mining Exchange (39 Exchange Place)

This Neo-Classical Revival, 2-story, T-shaped, sandstone building was constructed in 1908 to house a stock exchange. Organized in 1888, the exchange dealt almost exclusively in mining and petroleum stock and operated by open auction system. In 1897 seats sold for $16; two years later they sold for $400. The exchange was busy trading uranium stocks through the 1950s. Exchange Place takes its name from this building which now accommodates attorneys and architects. The building was designed by non-Mormon architect John Craig. National Register of Historic Places.

To your left (south), with the cast iron lamps and bands of colorful mosaic tiles, is the Commercial Club building.

30. Commercial Club (32 Exchange Place)

This impressive 6-story Second Renaissance Revival building was constructed in 1909 at a cost of nearly $400,000 and was intended by its architects, Ware and Treganza, as a smaller version of the New York City Athletic Club. Its polychromatic terra-cotta inlaid panels of colorful mosaics make it easily one of the most attractive commercial structures in the downtown area. Notice the decorative eaves, lions' heads above the ornate keystones, and winged head of Mercury above the door. Originally the building boasted a lounge, game rooms, ladies' parlor, banquet room, and private dining areas. A basement swimming pool is no longer used. Today the building houses a private nightclub and offices.

Further west, on your right (north), is the Boston building.

31. Boston Building (15-17 Exchange Place)

This 11-story commercial highrise was constructed in 1911. Designed by famous New York architect Henry Ives Cobb, it has a distinctive eastern urban look. Financed by Samuel Newhouse and named after his Boston Consolidated Mine Company, it contributed to his dream of a miniature Wall Street in Salt Lake City. Notice the three-part design—main floors, vertical office floors, and massive cornice—which imitate the base, shaft, and capital of a classical column. Also notice that the huge coat-of-arms shields (cartouches) under the second-story dentiled cornice are replicated at the top of the building.

Directly south of the Boston building through the courtyard, in matching style, is another office building, the Newhouse. These twin office buildings were Utah's first skyscrapers.

Commercial Club (I.30)

32. Newhouse Building (10 Exchange Place)

Samuel Newhouse made his multi-million-dollar fortune in freighting and mining. Raised in New York City by Russian-Jewish immigrants, he earned a law degree there before heading west and is said to have been successful in part because of his flamboyance. He and his wife Ida typified the frenetic 1890s, shuttling between mansions in Salt Lake City, Long Island, London, and Paris. After a number of financial reversals, Newhouse was forced into bankruptcy, and he and Ida separated in 1915. Newhouse then lived for a few years in his nearby Newhouse Hotel but eventually left for Paris, where he died in 1930. Ida lived in the Belvedere Apartments before she moved to the Beverly Hills Hotel.

Like the Boston building, the Newhouse is a stone-faced, steel-framed structure with classical details. It would be well worth taking a moment to study the carved stonework at the upper level, especially the industrial and agricultural symbols, including a garland of corn stocks. Also notice the copper corner window frames on the ground level; inside is a marble staircase and copper mail drop.

Continue west a few steps to Main Street. From here you can see the Frank Moss Federal Court House across the street to the west.

33. United States Court House (350 South Main Street)

Completed in 1906, this $500,000 Neo-Classical Revival building is the oldest in the district. The classical style was popular for government buildings during this era. Originally used as the Federal Building and Post Office, and significantly remodeled and enlarged in the 1930s, the building is now used only for judicial purposes. It was recently renamed after former Utah senator Frank Moss. Besides the imposing columns, notice the stone balustrade extending the length of the roof.

From here turn left (south) and walk to the first building south of the Newhouse building.

34. New Grand Hotel (369 South Main Street)

This 5-story brick building was constructed in 1910 for John Daly with money earned by the Daly-Judge mines in Park City, Utah. Notice the bracketed, projecting cornice, colorful inlaid tile panels, and carved stone buffaloes' heads. It was refurbished in 1990 and converted to low-income housing, with a restaurant occupying the ground level and a private club around the corner in the basement. Daly also owned the Moxum Hotel, was president of the Alta Club, and helped finance construction of the Cathedral of the Madeleine.

At 400 South Street, head west (right) across Main Street and walk nearly to the end of the block.

Across the street to your left, now a parking lot, was the Hotel New-house (400 South Main Street), a spectacular 11-story, 300-room hotel with a replica of the Louis XV Room at Versailles. It gradually declined and was demolished in the 1980s.

To your right, after the court house parking lot, Diamond Plaza, and a pub, is the V-shaped, 3-story, brick Shubrick Hotel.

35. Shubrick Hotel (72 West 400 South Street)

Built in 1912 for Blanche and Archibald Rykdert who were involved in Utah's mining industry, the Shubrick has operated continuously as an apartment house and hotel and retains much of its original character and integrity. Notice the rich effect of the polychromatic scheme. The gazebo-trellis that tops the central courtyard area at the second-floor level is especially interesting.

Continue west to the corner of West Temple Street. From here, notice the building diagonally across the street on the southwest corner advertising The Bay dance club. This was the Eagles Club lodge.

36. Eagles Club (404 South West Temple Street)

Built in 1916 for the Fraternal Order of Eagles, Aerie 67, this restored building now houses a non-alcoholic dance club and patio swimming pool. Among other things, you can see Beaux Arts pineapples in the surface decoration. The lodge was designed by N. Edward Liljenberg.

Turn right, head north on West Temple Street, and walk half a block to Market Street (340 South). Across the street to the northwest (328 South West Temple Street) you can see the red-brick structure originally housing the Chinese Social Center in the Bing Kung Tong Benevolent Association building (founded 1919).

At Market Street, turn right. The New York Hotel is halfway down the block on the left (north) side.

37. New York Hotel (48 Market Street)

This 75-room hotel was built in 1906 for Orange Salisbury, a Cornell-educated mining engineer who obtained several patents and organized the Kelly Filter Press Company. Although the façade is relatively simple, the horizontality and central parapet roof-line enhance the overall feeling of elegance. Following extensive renovations in the mid-1970s, the building now houses offices, a restaurant, and two private clubs, including the elegant New Yorker Club downstairs to the west (a temporary membership is available). At ground level is the private Market Street Oyster Bar and the public Market Street Grill. National Register of Historic Places.

Ahead to your right (south) is a brick and rusticated-stone building that once housed the fraternal lodge of the Independent Order of Odd Fellows (I.O.O.F.).

38. Odd Fellows Hall (39 Market Street)

This meeting hall was constructed in 1891. Considering the rich symbolism available for exterior decor and the amount of surface detail, the single fraternal symbol—the all-seeing eye—carved in stone over the main entrance is surprising. Still, decorative metalwork abounds on the cornice levels and capitals of the cast-iron columns. Notice that the building's Romanesque façade is nicely textured. National Register of Historic Places.

In the late nineteenth century the development of exclusive societies coincided with the growth of Utah's non-Mormon population. The quasi-religious nature of fraternal organizations generally meant that Mormons and Catholics were excluded. For local Protestants and Jews who comprised the bulk of fraternal membership, participation offered social benefits, life insurance policies, and other amenities.

Continue east to Main Street, noticing the decorative copper cornices of the Boston and Newhouse buildings ahead of you. The Felt building is directly across Main Street, next door (north) to the Boston building.

39. Felt Building (341 South Main Street)

This elegant commercial building, erected in 1909 by Orange Salisbury, was named for Charles Felt, one of the executives of the Salisbury Investment Company and a member of the anti-Mormon American Party. Although technically not a skyscraper, this tall Sullivanesque office building is five stories. Richard Kletting's design includes a terra-cotta façade, a dentilled cornice decorated with blossoms, and relief portraits of classical Greek figures in the arches above the top windows. Also notice the newly restored ground level façade. National Register of Historic Places.

Turn left and walk north to the corner (300 South). Across the street to your right, on the southeast corner, is the Judge building, also known as the Railroad Exchange.

40. Judge Building (8 East 300 South Street)

Mary Judge constructed this 7-story "fire-proof" building in 1907 as offices for twenty-two railroad companies. Although the commercial style architecture is rather straightforward, the copper cornice is remarkable. Be sure to notice the interesting detail at the southwest corner of the building. It is also worth noting that on the sixth floor in 1985, Mormon document dealer Mark Hofmann killed collector Steven Christensen with a pipebomb to prevent exposure as a forger.

Mary Harney, of Irish descent, married Irish immigrant John McBrehoney who changed his name to Judge when he arrived in the United States. John was a partner with Thomas Kearns and David Keith in the Silver King Mine in Park City and worked six days a week, seeing Mary only on Sundays, dying of dust inhalation in 1892. Mary subsequently invested dividends in real estate, endowed the Catholic high school on 1100 East Street which bears her name, and contributed toward construction of the Cathedral of the Madeleine. National Register of Historic Places.

Across the street to the northwest is the Clift building. Before crossing the street, notice the decorative window balconies on the eighth floor supported by scrolled brackets and topped by Greek pediments. Cross 300 South Street to the north.

41. Clift Building (10 West 300 South Street)

This impressive building was constructed in 1920 by Virtue Clift in honor of her late husband, Francis, a mining entrepreneur, whom she married when she was sixteen years old. The building was erected on the site of the old Clift Hotel. At nine stories, this is one of the largest terra-cotta-faced buildings in Salt Lake City. Notice how the vertical sweep is interrupted by horizontal banding typical of Second Renaissance Revival buildings. National Register of Historic Places.

East of the Clift Building across Main Street is the $100-million 24-story American Stores office tower scheduled for completion in 1998.

Continue north to Sam Weller's Zion Bookstore, mid-block, located in the Keith building on the west side.

42. Keith Building (256 South Main Street)

Built in 1902 at a cost of $150,000, this 3-story building first housed the Keith-O'Brien Company dry goods store. David Keith and lifelong friend Thomas Kearns discovered the Silver King vein in Park City which produced $10 million in gold, silver, and lead. Keith and Kearns purchased the *Salt Lake Tribune* in 1905, and Keith was president of numerous banks, railroads, and fraternities, and a member of Utah's constitutional convention. The building was designed by Alta Club architect Frederic Hale. The brick is faced in gray stone, and there are a number of window treatments and classical features. Although primarily flat, the building is divided into three vertical sections, and if you can see the upper levels, you can tell that the overall effect was pleasing. Weller's bookstore has been in business sixty-five years, in the present location since 1961. National Register of Historic Places.

Continue north to the Lollin building.

43. Lollin Building (238 South Main Street)

John Lollin, a Danish immigrant, operated the popular Lollin Saloon at 129 South Main Street. He financed this building in 1894 to house the Hudson Bay Fur Company and Ella Becker Millinery; he lived in a third-floor apartment. The bottom level has been altered, but the Neo-Classical arches, columns, and dentilled cornice are still visible in the upper levels. The stone foundation and brick frame are faced with gray plaster scored to look like stone. National Register of Historic Places.

Continue north.

44. Karrick Hall (236 South Main Street)

Lewis Karrick's 1887 gambling hall included apartments for eight prostitutes upstairs, several of whose names remain on their doors (not open to the public). Karrick founded the National Bank of the Republic which financed other brothels on Commercial Street. He also headed

Lollin Building (I.43)

Karrick Hall (I.44)

the local vigilante Karrick Guards. He made an unsuccessful bid for mayor on the Liberal Party ticket. When his fortune dwindled, and following a series of illnesses, he committed suicide in 1905.

The Lollin and Karrick buildings were designed by Richard Kletting, Utah's most prominent late nineteenth-century architect. Kletting was versatile. He was competent in classical, Romanesque, and Victorian architecture, and, best known for his state capitol design, he seems to have enjoyed the playful diversion offered here. Although the building is only 30-feet wide, he produced a textured façade displaying numerous mediums (including carved stone) and an interesting use of positive and negative space evident in the ornamental pilasters and window recesses. The ground-level floor has since been modified. National Register of Historic Places.

Continue north to West One Bank on your left at the southwest corner, formerly the National Bank of the Republic.

45. National Bank of the Republic (208 South Main Street)

This stone-and-brick veneered Second Renaissance bank is one of the earliest steel and concrete structures to mark the Salt Lake City skyline. Notice the decorative relief portraits in the keystones above the arched windows, the relief blossoms in the entrance archway, and the simulated balcony at the third level below the corbeled windows. The building was constructed in 1923 for the National Bank of the Republic, which financed many of the brothels, saloons, and gambling halls in town. It was constructed on the site of the "White House," an early hotel popular with visitors at the turn of the century. Local financier James Cosgriff subsequently consolidated several banks to form Continental National Bank and Trust, recently purchased by West One Bank. Cosgriff's son Walter later clashed with federal regulators who accused him of giving loans to "anything that can swim, creep, run, or fly." National Register of Historic Places.

Immediately west on 200 South Street stood the Cullen Hotel (33 West), whose bar and lobby became a club for cattle men and miners. It was designed by Richard Kletting and built in 1891, then razed in 1954.

The intersection where you stand is famous as the spot where inventor Lester Wire installed America's first electric traffic signal. It looked like a birdhouse and was ridiculed as "Wire's pigeon house." People initially resisted the concept of waiting for a light when there was little traffic, but the idea gradually caught on.

Cross to the Walker Bank on the northeast corner of 200 South, the building with eagles surrounding the railing on top of the penthouse tower.

46. Walker Center (175 South Main Street)

When completed in 1912, this 16-story commercial style building was the tallest between Chicago and San Francisco. Built of steel, concrete, and brick, it also features considerable terra-cotta ornamentation. Walker Brothers Bankers was the first banking establishment in Utah Territory.

The four Walker brothers established a mercantile business in 1859, selling provisions to Johnston's Army stationed at Camp Floyd southwest of the city. When Brigham Young founded ZCMI, the Walkers sided with the Godbeite dissenters and were excommunicated. Their business continued to thrive, however, as few were able to pass up the lure of eastern imports.

Walker Brothers Dry Goods began negotiating loans in a back room where their iron safe held gold dust and coins. They eventually owned mines, hotels, an opera house, and interest in railroads and factories. The dry goods firm declined, but the bank thrived.

The rooftop cupola is illuminated at night in blue when the weather is fair, red during a storm, flashing red when a storm approaches, and flashing blue for a fair-weather forecast. Notice how the corner window frames give the illusion of depth.

Next door to the north is the Herald building. It appears to be two twin towers but is U-shaped.

47. Herald Building (165 South Main Street)

This 5-story commercial building was constructed in 1905 for the *Salt Lake Herald*, founded in 1870 as a pro-Mormon newspaper sympathetic to Democrats. It ceased publication in 1920. The open space in the middle of the two towers is a light well that would normally be found at the rear of the building. Notice the elaborate metal cornice, the curve behind the light well, and lions in the frieze. Below the lions, at ground level, is Lamb's restaurant, which has occupied the ground floor since 1919. National Register of Historic Places.

Continue next door to the north.

48. First National Bank (163 South Main Street)

Built in 1871, this is the oldest cast-iron façade in the Intermountain West (now partially boarded over), and was designed by Richard M. Upjohn, namesake son of the famous New York architect. Originally called Miners National Bank, the institution was founded in 1866 by Charles Dahler, agent for Ben Holladay's Overland Mail and Express stage route, and gold and land broker Warren Hussey. In 1875 it was shortened one story by fire and given a new roof. The building then became a Masonic temple (the third-floor assembly room and glass-paneled partitions in the library still exist). In the 1880s it became the offices of later governor Simon Bamberger. Not open to the public. National Register of Historic Places.

Continue north two buildings, past the Beaux Arts Hepworth Carthey building to the Tracy building.

49. Tracy Loan and Trust Building (151 South Main Street)

This Neo-Classical Revival bank was constructed in 1916 for Russell

Herald Building (I.47)

Lord Tracy. Although small in scale (thirty feet high), the bank is a showcase of classical details, including ionic columns, a traditional Greek entablature, dentils, and an egg-and-dart banding.

Tracy's company was founded in 1884 in Cheyenne but moved to Salt Lake City in 1892. Among Tracy's legendary philanthropic ventures are a boy scout camp in Millcreek Canyon and an aviary at Liberty Park. Every Thanksgiving he invited the city's paperboys to dine with his family at the Tracy mansion. National Register of Historic Places.

Continue three buildings north.

50. Ezra Thompson Building (143 South Main Street)

The *Mormon Tribune,* now the *Salt Lake Tribune,* was founded in 1870 by Mormons unhappy with Brigham Young's blending of church and state. They employed *New York Herald* reporter Oscar Sawyer as chief editor, and the paper turned a critical eye on local culture. This was a hit among sophisticates but loathed by rank and file Mormons. The original offices were on 100 South Street, but relocated to the Thompson building in 1937. Notice the continuous piers and terra-cotta cornice suggestive of early Art Deco styling.

Before the Thompson building was erected in 1924, the historic Salt Lake House stood here. At this hotel in 1859 a member of cattle-rustler Cub Johnson's gang shot and maimed rival outlaw Bill Hickman. When an accomplice stormed Hickman's room, a revolver in each hand, Hickman's guard stabbed him eleven times with a bowie knife. Four years later at the same hotel, the same guard fatally stabbed one of Johnson's group, this time in the presence of witnesses. He was arrested and executed, signaling the demise of Hickman's "hounds." During the Utah War two "spies" were held at the Salt Lake House until shot. This is also where *Atlantic Monthly* correspondent Fritz Ludlow interviewed gunslinger Orrin Porter Rockwell in 1862.

North of the *Tribune* building on the southeast corner of 100 South Street is where Mormon schismatic leader William Godbe's 3-story Godbe, Pitts & Co. building stood, with the Godbe-Pitt Drugstore on the main level and physicians and dentists above.

Directly opposite the *Tribune* building to the west, beside the Utah Theatre's marquee, are the Kearns and Daft buildings. You can see them best from this (east) side of the street.

51. Kearns Building (136 South Main Street)

A magnificent building completed in 1911 for Thomas Kearns, this 10-story "skyscraper" is the best preserved Sullivanesque highrise in the intermountain west. The style, developed by Louis Sullivan, was employed by Los Angeles architects Parkinson and Bergstrom. The Kearns building was constructed of concrete with a terra-cotta façade facing the street and brick façades on the sides. Windows are set in recessed, arched, vertical rows. The prominent cornice jutting out from the roof, and terra-cotta statues and ornamentation, add visual interest.

Kearns Building (I.51)

Kearns Building, detail (I.51)

Kearns Building, detail (I.51)

Most striking are the seven life-size female figurines supporting lanterns at the second-story level. They are said to bear the face of Kearns's daughter. National Register of Historic Places.

Kearns was a Utah mining entrepreneur, U.S. senator, and part-owner of the *Mormon Tribune*. He contributed toward construction of the Cathedral of the Madeleine and St. Ann's Orphanage. From 1911 until his death he served on the board of trustees of Catholic University of America.

Next door to the north is the Daft building.

52. Daft Building (128 South Main Street)

The best surviving example of the work of Elias Harrison, a Mormon dissenter, this Victorian Queen Anne façade over a brick base fronted Sarah Daft's real estate office at the turn of the century. Four stories tall, it was completed in 1890 at a cost of $17,500. Notice the interesting detailing, blending of materials (brick, sandstone, and wood), and the movement in and out—especially the cantilevered windows. The Young Men's Literary Association, an alternative to Mormon youth programs, met on the second floor beginning in 1864. In 1908 the building was acquired by John Daynes, an English watchmaker, for Daynes Jewelry and Music companies. Daynes served thirty years as Mormon Tabernacle organist. National Register of Historic Places.

After viewing the Kearns and Daft buildings from this side of the street (east), cross Main Street to the west, turn right, and walk past these two structures north to the corner of 100 South Street. The building on your left with the terra-cotta eagle over the entrance and a four-faced, 120-year-old brass clock in front is the Eagle Emporium.

53. Eagle Emporium (102 South Main Street)

The oldest commercial building in downtown Salt Lake City, the Eagle Emporium was constructed in 1863 to house William Jennings's general mercantile business. It became the original home of ZCMI in 1868 when still a single story, then Zion's First National Bank in 1890. In 1916 the bank had the stone building refaced with a Neo-Classical veneer of terra-cotta. Notice the dignity and stability implied by the façade, camouflaging the building's small scale.

Jennings immigrated from England when he was twenty-six years old, working as a butcher (his father's trade) and tanner before earning his first million. He made his fortune first as a freighter and then supplying grain to the Overland Stage Company, investing profits in railroading and banking. Jennings also served as a director of Deseret National Bank. A devout Mormon, he had two wives. The building's original architect was Jennings's father-in-law, William Paul, who also designed Jennings's Devereaux House mansion.

From this corner, notice First Security Bank diagonally across the street on the northeast corner.

54. First Security Bank (79 South Main Street)

Built during World War I, First Security Bank grew out of the Bank of Deseret organized in 1871 by the only Mormon bankers at the time, William Hooper and Horace Eldredge. When Brigham Young socialized Mormon businesses, the bank became Zion's Cooperative Banking Institution, which spawned Zion's Savings Bank and Trust (now Zion's First National Bank). A smaller imitation of the Walker Bank building, it rises fourteen stories and includes all the basic stylistic elements of a commercial skyscraper. The words "Deseret Building" are preserved in raised letters over the west entrance.

Cross the street to the north. The McCornick and Company Bank is on the northwest corner.

55. McCornick and Company Bank (78 South Main Street)

Constructed of sandstone and brick in 1890, this 7-story building housed the largest private bank between St. Louis and San Francisco. When the bank was later purchased by Walker Brothers, the building was leased as office space. The smoothly dressed stone façade lends dignity but is unusually austere for the effusive Romanesque Revival period. The building represents the transitional period before the advent of skyscrapers. National Register of Historic Places.

William McCornick was born in Ontario, dabbled in ranching and mining in California, and moved to Utah Territory in 1873 to found the Lucky Boy Mining Company. He helped found the Alta Club, was its first president, and founded the Salt Lake City Chamber of Commerce. He was a director of Consolidated Wagon and Machine Company, Utah-Idaho Sugar (U & I), and Utah Power and Light, as well as president of the State Agricultural College. A Presbyterian and Republican, McCornick managed to maintain a working relationship with Mormons who were predominately Democrats. His building is the site of the retail outlet for Kimball and Lawrence importers.

Just north of the McCornick building is the Sullivanesque McIntyre building.

56. McIntyre Building (68-72 Main Street)

This 8-story highrise is built of steel-reinforced and poured concrete, with metal-framed windows. It was designed by Richard Kletting and constructed in 1909 as an office building for William McIntyre. The continuous piers running from ground level to cornice emphasize the building's height. This is the earliest and purest example of Sullivanesque architecture in the state. National Register of Historic Places.

McIntyre and brother Samuel came to Utah from Texas where their father had fought at the Alamo. The two sons established themselves in the cattle drive business, then William struck it rich prospecting the Tintic Mining District (named after Chief Tintic) southwest of Salt Lake City, exploiting the seemingly inexhaustible Mammoth Mine.

Continue north one block and you will be at Temple Square. This concludes the Salt Lake City Downtown Business District tour.

II.
Downtown Entertainment District

DISTANCE: 2.5 MILES   TIME: 3 HOURS

Begin at the 515-room Marriott Hotel (75 South West Temple Street). You can park either at the Marriott or next door to the north at Crossroads Plaza where your parking will be validated should you decide to shop there.

1. Marriott Hotel (75 South West Temple Street)

Utah native J. Willard Marriott started in business with 9-seat root beer stands before expanding to hotels and airline catering. Marriott was a devout Mormon who donated lavishly to Utah institutions, including Brigham Young University and the University of Utah. Copies of the Book of Mormon are placed in nearly all Marriott Hotel rooms worldwide.

Walk south along West Temple Street and across 100 South Street to the old glass and paint factory to the left (east) of the Mikado restaurant (located in the old "Kimball Block").

2. Bennett Glass and Paint Company (65 West 100 South Street)

The west section of this building was constructed in 1896 for the firm of Sears and Liddle. In 1921 John F. Bennett built the east section, matching and doubling the first bay, as is evident by the seam between the original building and expansion. Construction dates are engraved in the masonry. The company's skill in art glass manufacturing is evident in the building's leaded glass windows. Bennett's company was the largest paint and stained glass window producer in the state. Bennett also served as vice-president and general manager of ZCMI and vice-president of Utah State National Bank.

Two buildings east, with glass brickwork, is the Dinwoodey furniture building, now occupied by a branch of Zion's Credit Corporation.

3. Dinwoodey Building (37 West 100 South Street)

The Dinwoodey Cabinet Shop moved here from Main Street in 1869. The founder, Henry Dinwoodey, was a Mormon Scottish immigrant with three wives who parlayed Old World carpentry skills into the most prominent furniture supply house in the Intermountain West, eventually employing seventy-five workers. Because of the demand for burial caskets, Dinwoodey doubled as an undertaker. The original building was a 2-story adobe structure which was expanded to three stories in 1873. The current 6-story structure, built in 1890, has a flat façade that unfortunately covers a wonderfully flamboyant Victorian front.

41

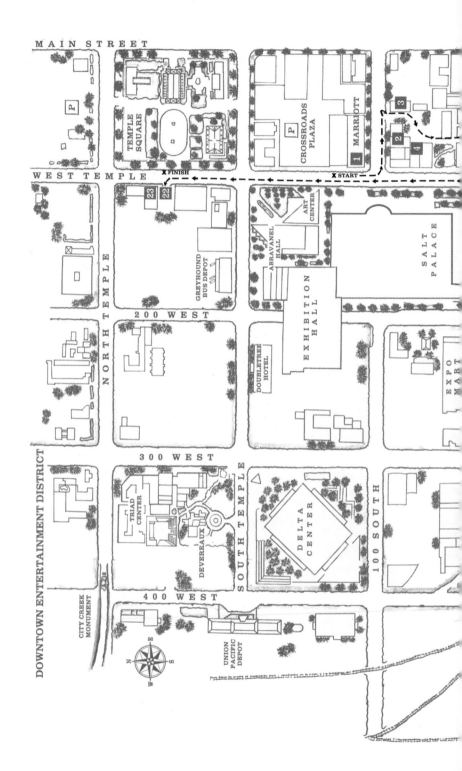

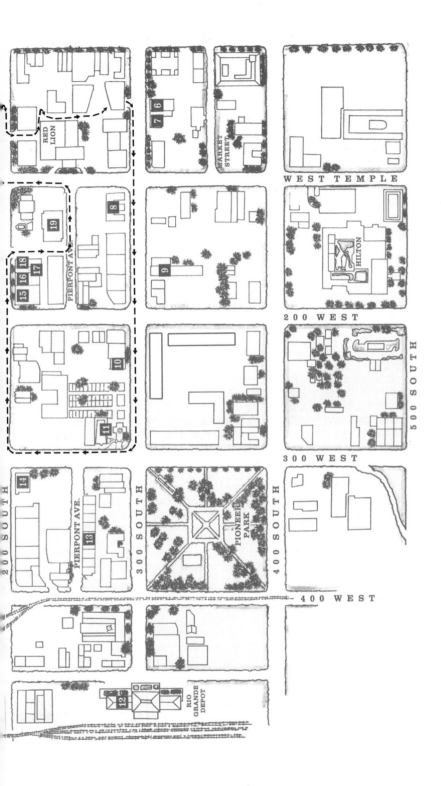

RED LION

7 6

MARKET STREET

WEST TEMPLE

8

19

18
16
17
15

PIERPONT AVE.

9

HILTON

200 WEST

500 SOUTH

10

11

300 WEST

14

PIERPONT AVE.

13

300 SOUTH

PIONEER PARK

400 SOUTH

200 SOUTH

400 WEST

12

RIO GRANDE DEPOT

Between the Bennett and Dinwoodey buildings is Dinwoodey Plaza, now leased by neighboring Cafe Molisse. Walk south and west through the plaza. The mural on the Dinwoodey building is of Double Arch in Utah's Arches National Park. Dinwoodey Plaza closes at 6:00 p.m.

Exit through the southwest corner of the plaza into the alley and turn right and then left into the passageway through the building housing the Dead Goat Saloon on the left (east) and the Arrow Press building on the right. The saloon opened in 1965.

4. Arrow Press Building (165 South West Temple Street)

The Tribune Reporter Printing Company, later called Arrow Press, erected this building in 1890. It is now a popular spot for restaurants and private clubs.

As you emerge from the passageway into Arrow Press Square, follow the brick-paved walkway south past the Utah Power and Light West Temple substation (on your left), along Restaurant Row between Benihana of Tokyo on the left and the cement-and-glass GTE Health Systems office building and parking tower to the right, to 200 South Street.

At 200 South Street, turn left (east) to see the Orpheum (now Capitol) Theatre.

5. Orpheum Theatre (50 West 200 South Street)

Constructed in 1913 by the Orpheum vaudeville theater chain, this stage opened eight years after its sister Orpheum two blocks east on State Street. San Francisco architect Albert Lansburgh conceived the elaborate Italian Renaissance façade in polished granite and polychromatic terra-cotta. Notice the lamp-bearing cherubs, lion's-head water spouts lining the cornice, and Palladian windows (tripartite, arched in the center). A 1909 marquee spanned the width of 200 South Street from sidewalk to sidewalk, and can now be found at the north entrance to Trolley Square (650 East 500 South).

The theater's interior included the latest in structural design. There were no view-obstructing pillars, the lights were concealed, and acoustical considerations were finely tuned. In 1927 the interior was renovated for motion pictures, then restored in 1976 to house the Utah Opera Company, Ballet West, Ririe-Woodbury Modern Dance Company, and Repertory Dance Theatre. National Register of Historic Places.

Backtrack west to the crosswalk mid-block. Cross 200 South Street to the statue "Counterpoint" by Dennis Smith and continue south between American Plaza I and American Plaza II, past the Plaza North Amphitheater, to the red lion logo on the north wall of the Red Lion Inn.

Turn left and proceed a few steps east, to the northeast corner of the inn where you will find an American Plaza directory. Turn right and walk south between American Plaza III and Red Lion Inn. Continue south, with American Towers North condominiums on your left, to the

Orpheum Theatre (II.5)

Orpheum Theatre, detail (II.5)

outdoor patio surrounded by six flags. Exit by descending the stairs (southeast of the flags) to 300 South Street (or Broadway) through American Towers South.

Notice the two buildings across the street.

6. Greenewald Furniture Company (35 West 300 South Street)

Now offices for Family Health Program (FHP), Greenewald Furniture was the first company to occupy Mary Judge's 4-story unreinforced brick commercial structure. Built in 1903, it was later a millinery mall housing Forbes Hat, Jay Hat, and Bercu Millinery. National Register of Historic Places.

Next door to the west is the Ely Hotel.

7. Ely Hotel (43 West 300 South Street)

One of a number of hotels built during the first two decades of the twentieth century near the railroad depots, this narrow, 3-story hotel, built in 1906 by wagon and plough dealer James Paine, now houses an antique shop. In 1920 Paine sold the building to Salt Lake Stamp Company which moved into the ground level four years later but kept the hotel in operation on the upper floors. A later occupant was Thousand Peaks Livestock Company.

Turn right and head west on 300 South Street to the corner of West Temple Street, noticing the Zephyr private nightclub to your left on the southeast corner with glass brick (301 South West Temple). Check the marquee for the current live bands performing there.

Cross West Temple Street to the west. The Peery Hotel is on the northwest corner.

8. The Peery Hotel (110 West 300 South Street)

This elegant 3-winged Prairie-School building was constructed in 1910 for Joseph and David Peery. They sold the hotel in 1947 to Harry Miles who owned the Showboat Hotel in Las Vegas. The hotel was restored in 1985 to include a popular pub and cafe. Notice how the warm cream-colored brick and classical details create an inviting exterior. National Register of Historic Places.

Continue west along the north side of 300 South Street. On your right is the new Rose Wagner Performing Arts Center. Notice Squatter's Pub Brewery (147 West) across the street to the south in the old Garden Hotel, built in 1909. Squatter's produces its own lager, stout, and ale and is open to the public.

Next door, west of Squatter's, is the McDonald Chocolate Company building.

9. J. G. McDonald Chocolate Company (159 West 300 South Street)

Combining elements of commercial and Sullivanesque styles, this 4-story chocolate factory was constructed in 1901 and an additional story added in 1914. Notice the different types of windows on each level, increasing in importance and interest to the top. Each day at noon workers took lunch in an elaborate roof garden among vines and flowers, monkeys, parrots, and hundreds of rare birds.

James McDonald inherited his father's business in 1912. It began as a grocery that manufactured its own saltwater taffy and hand-dipped chocolates. James began specializing in boxed chocolates and a chocolate drink intended to replace the "injurious use of tea and coffee." At its peak the company employed 400 people. The Dixon Paper Company moved into the building in 1941, and it is now artists' studios. National Register of Historic Places.

Continue west, passing the former site of Bandaloops private club (176 West) on your right, the site of Utah's first Mormon Sunday school. As you walk, notice the street lamps which date from the early 1900s.

Cross 200 West Street, proceeding west on 300 South Street to the Broadway Hotel, on your right, with the portico extending over the sidewalk.

10. Broadway Hotel (222 West 300 South Street)

Built in 1912 for Samuel and David Spitz, the Broadway is now a tenement hotel. Although the brown brick is monochromatic, the bricks on the upper level are laid in rectangular panes, and the spandrels and rusticated pilasters create additional interest. National Register of Historic Places.

Across the street opposite the Broadway is the site of the earliest city cemetery, now Palladio apartment development. The graves have been moved to This Is The Place State Park (formerly Pioneer Trail State Park).

Continue west, passing quaint Delmar and Wayne courts (240 and 250 West) on your right, to the cathedral on the northeast corner of 300 West and 300 South streets, a loose replica of St. Sophia's in Istanbul.

11. Holy Trinity Greek Orthodox Church (279 South 300 West Street)

This Byzantine cathedral—built like a basilica with a central dome and two side wings—was completed in 1924. The rich gold brick is complemented by stone arches and tile work below two domed bell towers. The effect is a stunning statement to the faith of this people. The impressive stained glass windows and interior murals depict important New Testament themes. Dedicated in 1924, the sanctuary served as the nucleus of Greek Town, famous for its coffee houses. Enclaves of Finns, Italians, Slavs, Syrians, and Japanese also lived in the area. Locally Greeks comprised the largest ethnic component on railroad, mine, mill, and smelter rolls. A Memorial Hall was added in 1950 on the north side. National Register of Historic Places.

Holy Trinity is the last remnant of immigrant life in the city. Italian import and grocery stores are gone. An early Catholic church was torn down to make way for a freeway to the south, and the entire Japanese district was demolished when the Salt Palace convention center was built.

From this corner, notice Pioneer Park diagonally across the street to the southwest, where the pioneer fort and several log and adobe houses were erected in 1847. The park now serves as an unofficial refuge for the city's transient and homeless population and is also a farmers' market during the late summer. The palatial Denver and Rio Grande train depot (300 South Rio Grande Street) looms in the distance further west. To the west and north of the train depot are a number of soup kitchens. Use caution in this area at night. You may want to simply view the depot from here, but if you decide to get a closer look, return to this corner to continue the tour.

12. Rio Grande Depot (300 South Rio Grande Street)

This landmark was constructed in 1909 for George Gould to service the Western Pacific Railroad. Combining elements of Beaux Arts classicism and Italian Renaissance, this edifice reaches far beyond function to create an inviting environment. Notice the huge arched windows that stretch three stories high. The interior is rich with light and color and is spatially interesting. Today the depot houses the Amtrak Station and Utah State Historical Society museum, library, and bookstore. In the north wing is the popular Rio Grande Cafe. Museum hours are Monday-Friday, 8:00 a.m.-5:00 p.m.

Originally the depot included a men's smoking room and women's retiring room. The depot is said to be haunted by a black-haired woman in purple velvet who was killed while retrieving an engagement ring that her boyfriend had thrown onto the tracks. National Register of Historic Places.

At the Greek Orthodox church (corner of 300 West and 300 South), head north past the Hellenic Memorial Cultural Center (on your right). To your left (west) across the street is a brightly colored mural on the east wall of the old Farmers' Market on Pierpont Avenue. The untitled mural was painted by Peruvian artist Peruko Copacatty in 1987.

You may want to cross the street to explore the art galleries and antique shops. If you do, return to this spot before continuing the tour.

13. Farmers' Market (325 West Pierpont Avenue)

Constructed in 1910 to house wholesale produce firms, one section later became a warehouse for Bradshaw Auto Parts where owner Franklin Bradshaw was murdered in 1978 by his grandson. Today's owner, Artspace, provides artists with affordable studios, living quarters, and backyard garden plots.

Continue north to 200 South. The Crane building is across the street to the west on the southwest corner.

14. Crane Building (307 West 200 South Street)

The Chicago-based Crane Company manufactured industrial valves and fittings, including beer barrel bushings and fire hydrants. The company constructed this 5-story box-shaped commercial building in 1910 in the city's warehouse district with the latest technology, including "fireproof" construction, a steel frame wall-bearing system, and an elevator sheathed with plaster blocks. The Westgate Business Center across the street to the northwest is a renovated warehouse of the same vintage.

Three blocks west is a famous city block, now owned by Utah Transit Authority, known as the "stockade" in the 1910s. This was a regulated red-light area, fenced and filled with "cribs"—small apartments just large enough for a bed and sink. The area has become somewhat gentrified through renovation of abandoned warehouses. Now restaurants, gay nightclubs, and small businesses attract people here.

From the corner where you are standing (200 South 300 West) you can see the 20,000-seat Delta Center to the northwest (300 West and South Temple Street), completed in 1991. Home to the Utah Jazz professional basketball team, the center includes 56 luxury suites, each of which features a private rest room, telephone, bar, refrigerator, microwave oven, television, and couch.

Across the street on the northeast corner are the Jackson Apartments (270 West), built in 1917 as the Fillmore and the Uintah, joined in 1946.

Turn right (east) and walk the length of the 200 South block to 200 West Street. On your left (north) is the ExpoMart which houses the downtown branch of the U.S. post office and trade-show arenas.

Cross 200 West Street to the east to the row of historic buildings beginning with the Smith-Bailey Drug warehouse (on your right), now First Commerce Center.

15. Smith-Bailey Drug Company (175 West 200 South Street)

The Syndicate Investment Company constructed this "up-to-date modern warehouse" in 1908 for $71,000. The most striking feature was the amount of glass and the arrangement of windows, but it bragged "fireproof" steel, freight elevators, and vaults.

Next door to the east is the Patrick building.

16. Patrick Building (163 West 200 South Street)

This 5-story commercial building was constructed in 1914 and housed the Decker-Patrick Company which was later renamed Patrick Dry Goods Company. The firm is still in business today providing wholesale fabric to retailers. Note the building's projecting cornice, striking color contrast, and interesting variation in window treatment. Next door to the east, now the Green Parrot private club, is what was once Hotel Victor.

17. Hotel Victor (155 West 200 South Street)

Erected in 1910 for Katherine Belcher, this 3-story hotel survived into the 1960s. Shortly after its construction it housed a saloon operated by Italian immigrants Alphonso Scovelli and Joseph Fratello. During the 1920s and 1930s the Denver Fire-Clay Company occupied the main floor where it manufactured fire brick and high-temperature clay, sold metallurgical and industrial furnaces, and dealt in heavy chemicals and laboratory equipment. The highly detailed façade combines a variety of motifs and has a high-contrast color scheme. National Register of Historic Places.

Continue past Marianne's Delicatessen (149 West)—a German cafe that has been in business over thirty-five years—to the Bertolini building.

18. Bertolini Building (145 West 200 South Street)

This Victorian Romanesque building, constructed in 1892 for Ignazio Bertolini, a prominent Italian real estate developer, has been occupied by various Italian, Greek, Russian, and Japanese businesses including a barber shop, restaurant, pool hall, organ grinder, and a variety of grocery stores. The rectangular plan, with the narrow end facing the street, was typical of small commercial buildings of the 1890s. National Register of Historic Places.

Turn right just past the Bertolini building and head south down the Pierpont walkway to Club Baci, a private club. Notice the word "heart" engraved in the walkway in over twenty languages and the fountain to the right simulating rain cascading off a roof.

Club Baci, on your left, is housed in the Oregon Shortline building.

19. Oregon Shortline Railroad Building (122 West Pierpont Avenue)

This was the first major work of architect Carl Neuhausen, who later designed the Kearns mansion, Cathedral of the Madeleine, and State Street Orpheum Theatre. The building was constructed in three stages beginning in 1897 to house Oregon Shortline railroad offices, then Salt Lake High School, and later the National Guard armory. Club Baci occupies what was once the gymnasium. Boxer Jack Dempsey is said to have trained here. The gymnasium is now decorated with local art and an impressive stained glass wall. National Register of Historic Places.

Continue south. When you reach Pierpont Avenue, notice the studios across the street housing architects, designers, artists, and a printing press.

Turn left (east), walking the length of the Oregon Shortline building (and adjacent parking terrace), and turn left onto West Temple Street. Walk north past the Shilo Inn (on your left), site of the famous 1894 Dooly building, demolished in 1961, which was the only structure in Utah designed by Louis Sullivan. The 6-story building housed the Alta Club and five architectural firms. Continue north to 200 South Street.

West Temple Street's checkered past includes an episode of city-sponsored prostitution. During the mid-1880s city officials and members of the police department collaborated in a vice sting directed at non-Mormon territorial officials as a payback for federal prosecution of

Mormon polygamists. Officials arranged for the purchase of two or three houses along this stretch of West Temple Street to which several prostitutes were given unrestricted access and offered a $300 reward for each territorial official compromised. Police informers were stationed at peepholes and served as state's witnesses in court. When details of the investigation were exposed, the Mormon-owned *Deseret News* defended the sting, but the non-Mormon *Daily Tribune* editorialized: "Salt Lake now enjoys the distinction of being the only city in the world in which houses of prostitution were established by the city authorities; the only city that ever hired official prostitutes and paid them a premium for every man they enticed. This city also has the only newspapers in the world that are vile enough to defend such infamy."

Cross 200 South Street to the north and continue past the Salt Lake Convention and Visitors Bureau on your left (180 South West Temple Street; open 8:00 a.m.-6:00 p.m. weekdays, 9:00 a.m.-4:00 p.m. Saturdays, closed Sundays) to the Salt Palace.

20. Salt Palace Convention Center (100 South West Temple Street)

The original Salt Palace was located at 900 South State Street and flaunted an ornate dome that looked like the top half of a gilded Christmas tree ornament. Before completion, the wood used in construction was sprayed with powdered salt under pressure to make the dome sparkle white—thus the name "Salt Palace." The idea was conceived by architect Richard Kletting. He placed the dome on top of a dignified, classical base. This fun house burned to the ground in 1910, eleven years after its opening.

A new $17-million palace emerged in 1969 and was considered an architectural achievement—its massive drumlike dome, now demolished, supported by tension cable. Following an $87-million "renovation," the new Salt Palace doubled its floor space to more than 250,000 square feet and opened in 1996 for trade shows and conventions.

As you continue north, notice the Hotel Albert across West Temple Street to the right (east) with the hanging chains-and-cement canopy.

21. Hotel Albert (165 South West Temple Street)

This 4-story Second Renaissance Revival hotel was constructed for Albert Fisher in 1909 at a cost of $100,000. Fisher, a German immigrant, owned Fisher Brewery and Hotel Plandome. Notice the carved stone of the façade and the metal cornice. Next to the hotel (north) stands the Arrow Press building, which we passed earlier. It houses Club DV8 which caters to a college-age crowd.

North of the Salt Palace, opposite Crossroads Plaza (east of you), is the Salt Lake Art Center (20 South West Temple Street), housing a 2-level gallery that features contemporary works by national and regional artists, a gift shop, and a lecture hall. During July and August it hosts free Twilight Concerts every Thursday evening on the lawn. The center is open Monday-Saturday, 10:00 a.m.-5:00 p.m.; Sunday, 1:00-5:00 p.m. Contributions are welcome.

North of the Art Center on the southwest corner of South Temple and West Temple streets, set back behind a promenade of fountains, is Maurice Abravanel Hall (123 West South Temple Street) where the Utah Symphony Orchestra performs. Part of a 1976 bicentennial arts complex, this hall has been widely hailed for its acoustics. Former conductor Abravanel, born in Greece and raised in Switzerland, received international praise for the symphony's recordings of Gustave Mahler's works. Mormon church president Wilford Woodruff's Valley House Hotel originally stood on this spot.

Across West Temple Street to the east, on the southeast corner, is the Inn at Temple Square (75 West South Temple Street), owned and operated by the LDS church. This is the site of the frontier Valley Tan Remedies factory which produced an elixir that promised to cure "rheumatism, headaches, diphtheria, cankers, and worms."

Three blocks west from the corner of South Temple and West Temple streets is the Union Pacific Railroad Station, which you can see in the distance. It is a bit of a hike to the depot, but, if you are up to it, follow the side trip directions. Otherwise cross South Temple Street to the north.

☞ Side Trip. Turn left and proceed west on South Temple Street. The Greyhound Bus Depot will be across the street to your right. At 200 West Street, cross to the Doubletree Hotel on the southwest corner and continue west another block. At 300 West Street (the Delta Center is on the southwest corner), cross to the northwest corner and continue west.

As you walk, notice the Triad Center business complex in the distance to your right, built in the early 1980s. Originally planned to cover twenty-four acres, this ambitious $600-million redevelopment project—which was to include a 4-level shopping center, three 25-story residential condominium towers, and a 600-room, 30-story hotel—fell on hard times in 1987 when Triad America, the holding company for Saudi businessman and arms merchant Adnan Khashoggi, filed bankruptcy. But the initial four buildings were completed, and the grounds are the setting for summer concerts and the Utah Arts Festival each June. Notice the fountains and sculpture by Janet Shapero with petroglyph designs etched in glass.

Mid-block on your right, set back from the street, is the Devereaux House (334 West South Temple Street), which began as a spacious cottage built by William Staines in 1857. Staines was Brigham Young's gardener and territorial librarian. His house was the site of truce negotiations between territorial governor Alfred Cumming and Brigham Young during the Utah War. Staines hosted British adventurer Richard Burton during his stay in Salt Lake City.

The house was purchased by a son of Brigham Young in 1865, and then by Utah's first millionaire, William Jennings, three years later. Jennings, Salt Lake City mayor 1882-85, was a devout Mormon with two wives. He expanded the house in 1868, adding the west pavilion, then replacing the cottage with a matching east pavilion in the late 1870s to give the house a Second Empire architectural look. He named the house after the Devereaux Estate in England where he was born. Jennings entertained such dignitaries as U.S. presidents Ulysses Grant and Rutherford Hayes. Following Jennings's death, the mansion became an office building as well as a rehabilitation center for alcoholics. The restored Second Empire mansion is now occupied by the Chart House Restaurant. National Register of Historic Places.

At the end of South Temple Street is the Union Pacific Railroad Depot (400 West). The $500,000 train depot was completed in 1909 by the Oregon Shortline as an example of French Second Empire architecture. The structure is built on piles because engineers believed the site was an old river bed. Notice the visual emphasis on the mansard roof. Also notice the gargoyles and stained glass windows. The vaulted waiting room contains Depression-era WPA murals depicting the driving of the golden spike at Promontory, Utah (connecting the Union Pacific to the Central Pacific railroads), and the entrance of pioneers into the valley. Originally the depot had separate waiting rooms for men and women. National Register of Historic Places.

From the railroad depot, walk north to the northwest corner of the Triad Center block. Under the viaduct you can see City Creek where it rises to the surface under North Temple Street. A pile of creek-bed boulders memorializes the creek, and a plaque on the east side of the boulders documents this period of Salt Lake City history.

To return to West Temple Street, walk east along the north side of the Triad Center to 300 West Street, cross to the east and continue two more blocks east. At West Temple Street, turn right. The first building on your right is the LDS Museum of Church History and Art, number 24 on the tour. End Side Trip.

———

If you did not take the side trip, continue north on West Temple Street past the LDS Family History Library on your left (35 North)—the largest genealogical library in the world and open to the public—to the log cabin set back from the street between the Family History Library and the LDS Museum of Church History and Art.

23. Deuel-Carrington Cabin

One of two surviving log cabins built by Mormon pioneers in 1847, the Deuel cabin was part of the north extension of the original Mormon pioneer fort. Constructed by Osmyn Deuel, a blacksmith, this single-cell structure was purchased two years later by Albert Carrington (a Mormon apostle from 1870 until his excommunication in 1885) who removed it to the corner of 100 North and West Temple streets. It was subsequently relocated to Temple Square and then placed in its current location.

North of the cabin, the granite-faced building with the modernist bas- relief is the Museum of Church History and Art.

24. Museum of Church History and Art (45 North West Temple Street)

The museum boasts a variety of changing displays featuring samples from the museum's 100,000-artifact collection. The concrete bas-relief was sculpted by Brigham Young University art professor Franz Johansen in a style influenced by Socialist Realism. It portrays scenes from LDS history, Mormon symbolism such as the tree of life, and prominent Mormon figures. Admission to the museum is free. Open weekdays 9:00 a.m.-9:00 p.m., weekends 10:00 a.m.-7:00 p.m.

The Marriott Hotel where you began the tour is directly south on West Temple Street and 100 South. This concludes the Downtown Entertainment District tour.

Museum of Church History and Art, interior (II.24)

III.
Capitol Hill and
City Creek Canyon

DISTANCE: 2.5 MILES   TIME: 3 HOURS

The hill overlooking Salt Lake City from the north was originally called Arsenal Hill after the Utah territorial arsenal which was located at the head of Main Street just inside the city wall. When another arsenal farther north blew up on 5 April 1876, the day before the semi-annual LDS general conference, citizens thought the U.S. army had launched a long-anticipated attack. After the State Capitol was constructed, the hill became known as Capitol Hill and today is among the oldest surviving residential areas in the city. The blocks are smaller here than elsewhere in the city, and streets follow the hillside contour. The western slope of the hill was once dotted with fruit orchards.

The earliest homes on the hill were built in the 1850s and 1860s using log and adobe. Foundations were made of red sandstone; roofs were shingled with cedar. The houses were rectangular, 1- and sometimes 2-story gabled structures set broadside to the street to give the illusion of greater size. During this early period houses were widely spaced and usually confined to the lower slopes of the hill. Later, dormer windows converted an extra half-story attic into sleeping space, and entranceways which opened directly to a kitchen were later modified with cross-wing additions which changed the houses into T- or L-shapes.

Later homes were higher, broader, and of various styles, but many retained the simplicity of the vernacular, Greek Revival, and Federal (the American architectural alternative to Georgian, named after King George) styles. The old city hall, where this tour begins, is a good example of Federal period architecture.

1. Old City Hall (300 North State Street)

Now Council Hall, this edifice was completed in 1866 and served as city hall and territorial capitol until 1894. Notice the square, symmetrical construction and dignified look of the sandstone, with simple ornamentation such as the octagonal cupola on top, the brackets under the roof eaves, the small balcony with pendants hanging from the corners, and the stone lintels on the side windows. It was designed by pioneer architect William Folsom. The 60-foot-square building was originally located at 120 East 100 South Street and was dismantled, coded, and moved block by block in 1962 to the hilltop where it now stands. The sandstone was quarried from nearby Red Butte Canyon. National Register of Historic Places.

Old City Hall (III.1)

Today Council Hall houses the Utah Travel Council and the Utah Tourism and Recreation Center which make available free information on Utah's public lands, including all national parks, national forests, and state parks. Open weekdays 8:00 a.m.-5:00 p.m.; weekends and holidays 10:00 a.m.-5:00 p.m.

Cross 300 North Street at the crosswalk directly north of the City Hall entrance, then veer to the left to the capitol promenade. Walk up the first flight of steps to the statue of Massassoit.

2. Chief Massassoit Monument (Capitol Hill)

Massassoit, famed Native American chief who welcomed early settlers in Massachusetts, was sculpted by noted Utah artist Cyrus Dallin who studied at the Academie Julian in Paris. Notice the bear motif on the peace pipe. A plaster mold of Massassoit originally stood inside the capitol. The statue was later recast in bronze and moved to its present location. It is ironic that an eastern rather than a local Native American was chosen for this spot, but when the original statue was commissioned for Plymouth Rock, the copy seemed like a windfall for Utah.

Continue north to the foot of the capitol steps, passing the monument to Union Pacific Railroad president Edward Harriman on the far left. Inheritance taxes on Harriman's estate helped finance construction of the capitol building.

On either side of the flagpole, between two blue spruces—Utah's state tree—are two copper beehives complete with bees.

3. Beehives and Time Capsule (Capitol Hill)

The beehive, which represents "industry," is Utah's state symbol. The time capsule was buried in 1991 with local memorabilia.

Enter the capitol building through the gold-colored metal doors at the top of the stairs.

4. Utah State Capitol Building (Capitol Hill)

The architect for this grand edifice was German-born Richard Kletting, educated in Munich, Vienna, and Paris. The design was inspired by the Maryland statehouse and Civil War-era U.S. capitol. Completed in 1915, this $2.7-million cement building with quartzite veneer is one of the best examples of Neo-Classical architecture in Utah. The copper-leaf dome—which has been shredded twice in hurricane-strength gales—tops a colonnade of twenty-four Corinthian columns. Notice the lantern on top of the massive dome. Other classical touches are the complex capitals of the lower columns (Ionic and Corinthian), the wide triangular pediment over the entrance (with copper lining), balustraded railings, and broken pediments over the windows of the upper drum.

The 165-foot high interior rotunda is of Georgian marble, which was preferred over Utah marble because of its lighter color. Between the arches, above recessed alcoves housing sculptures of historical figures, the walls are painted with murals of Utah's past—trapper and explorer

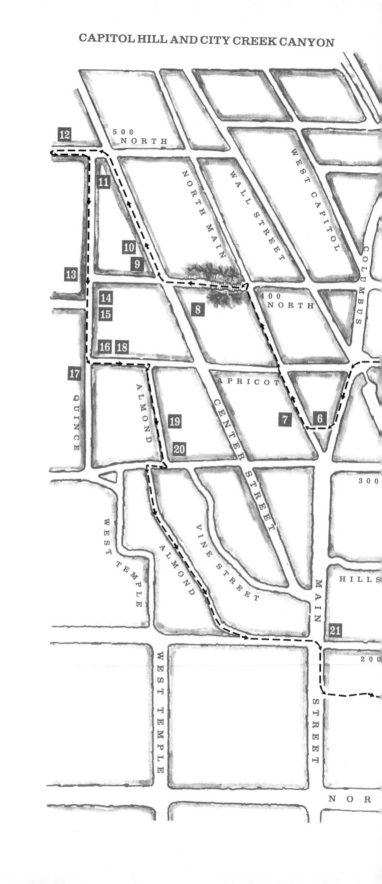

Peter Ogden discovering the Ogden River in 1628 (northeast corner), Catholic father Sylvester Velez de Escalante discovering Utah Lake in 1776 (southwest corner), U.S. surveyor John Fremont exploring the Great Salt Lake in 1843 (northwest corner), and Brigham Young viewing the Salt Lake Valley in 1847 (southeast corner).

On the floor of the rotunda are statues of Utah copper magnate Daniel Jackling (southwest end) and Brigadier General Thomas Kane (southeast end). Kane negotiated a settlement of the Utah War. Jackling was a philanthropist-playboy, and despite several attempts to replace his 9-foot copper-bronze statue in the rotunda with a statue honoring Brigham Young, he remains unmoved. A compromise was reached in 1994 with the placement of a statue of Young facing Kane and Jackling. There are also paintings of Utah's governors circling the outer walls.

The territorial and state legislatures occupied Social Hall, the City County Building, and Council Hall before the present capitol was finished. National Register of Historic Places. Open 8:00 a.m.-6:00 p.m. seven days a week, summer hours 6:00 a.m.-8:00 p.m.

Exit the rotunda to the west past the grand west staircase to the Gold Room (which cost $65,000 to decorate) on your left, which is open for viewing except during state receptions. The walls are marble with gold-leaf decoration. Notice the classical ceiling mural framed by relief cherubs.

Continue west and descend the small staircase. At the bottom of the stairs on your left is a memorial to the *USS Utah* which was sunk by Japanese fighter-bombers at Pearl Harbor in 1941. Proceed outside, walking west down the stairs and across two capitol driveways to the Vietnam War memorial at the bottom of the second set of stairs on your left.

5. Vietnam War Memorial (Capitol Hill)

Surrounded by trees and fronted by two flagpoles is the sculpture by Clyde Morgan of a soldier carrying his dead friend's rifle. Behind this 1989 statue is a commemorative wall listing Utahns who died in southeast Asia.

Continue west to Columbus Street. On the way you can see the Civil War, U.S. Constitution, and Pioneer monuments located across the lawn to the southwest. These commemorate a small group of mounted Utahns who served thirty days protecting telegraph lines at the outbreak of the Civil War, Mormons who enlisted in the war with Mexico to raise funds for immigration, and Mormon immigrants who died en route to Utah.

Head west across Columbus Street at the crosswalk leading to Apricot Avenue (345 North) and the string of Dutch Colonial Revival houses on the northwest corner of the intersection. These were built in 1903 by English-born druggist George Brice for his large family and tenants.

Turn left and proceed south on Columbus Street. To your right is the east side of the Pioneer Memorial Museum carriage house. Continue to the next building on your right, the museum's main building—noticing the buffalo skull reliefs on the east wall—and go to the south entrance.

6. Pioneer Memorial Museum (300 North Main Street)

Completed in 1950 by the Daughters of Utah Pioneers and the State of Utah, this 4-story edifice built on land leased to the DUP by the state is a loose replica of the old Salt Lake Theatre. During its nearly thirty years' planning and construction, the museum was the subject of some controversy regarding its placement at the top of North Main Street in a residential area without parking. In front of the museum is a statue of Eliza Snow, eulogized here as a Mormon "priestess" and remembered for her poem, "O My Father," which acknowledges a heavenly mother. Besides the imposing columns at the entrance, the museum has a decorative roof balustrade, not visible from your angle, which adds to the classical feel of the design.

Within the museum (no fee but contributions are welcome) are some thirty-seven rooms featuring a wide variety of artifacts from Utah's pioneer past, including the Salt Lake Theatre curtain and Brigham Young's carriage. To see the carriage, enter the lobby, turn right and descend the stairs to the basement level, where you can also see the wooden eagle from the original eagle gate located in the center of the room to your right. Proceed north through this display area, heading toward the far right doorway with a sign reading "Carriage House." Walk through this corridor, passing an old streetcar, fire engine, and covered wagon, to the staircase at the far left. At the top of the stairs, in the middle of the room, is Young's unrestored wagon. To exit, retrace your steps.

If you decide to browse further, you will find such treasures as Brigham Young's "blood stone" amulet designed to protect against evil spirits. The museum is open Mon.-Sat. 9:00 a.m.-5:00 p.m. (and Sunday afternoon during the summer).

Exit the museum, descend the stairs to your right, turn right, and walk north up North Main Street which runs along the west side of the museum. You are entering the Marmalade District, so named because of the orchards which once graced these hills and streets which were originally named after fruit-bearing trees. The houses here illustrate the ingenuity of eastern and European immigrants in adapting to a new climate and materials.

When city blocks were first laid out along the cardinal points of the compass, the entire central block (Temple Square) was considered to be the meridian rather than the southwest corner of the block. In the 1970s city planners corrected this, and house addresses north and west of Temple Square were changed. Some of the old curb markings remain and should be ignored. Follow street signs only.

As you continue north, notice the yellow-trimmed Box Style Thomas house across the street to your left (west).

Pioneer Memorial Museum (III.6)

7. Thomas House (331 North Main Street)

Houses on North Main Street are of a later period than others in the Marmalade District. This house was built in 1912 by James Thomas, a chemist. Notice the wide eaves and off-center front door indicative of Box Style architecture.

The door on the second level, which evidently leads to an unrailed balcony, is a vestige of pioneer architecture. Five possibilities for such apparently superfluous doors have been advanced: they allowed for a future balcony expansion, provided for escape in case of fire or heavy snow, allowed fresh air for occupants living upstairs before hinged and sliding windows became common, facilitated rug cleaning and moving upstairs furniture in and out, or provided an escape for polygamists during police raids.

Continue north, crossing Apricot Avenue. The Spanish Colonial Revival house on the northeast corner at 354 North Main was built in 1908 by Scottish immigrant Alexander McConachie. Up a few feet and across the street to your left (west) at 361 North Main is a one-room harness shop built in 1919 by blacksmith Willard Farnes.

The structure at 391 North Main looks as though it was a neighborhood store but in fact was real estate agent LeRoy Wight's 1904 cottage. Its original rock façade has been overlaid with stucco to give it a Pueblo Style look.

At 400 North, formerly Plum Street, cross the street to the west (left) and descend the stairs. At the bottom of the stairs, the T-shaped house to your left (south) before you reach the corner is the Jonasson home, with an attached carriage house.

8. Jonasson House (390 Center Street)

This pioneer house was built in 1872 by Sven Jonasson, an attorney and federal judge. He and his wife were handcart pioneers. Like other early homes with Gothic motifs, the gable side was built to face Center Street and the entrance moved to the back when the cross wing was added. Continue to the corner of Center Street and 400 North. The white-painted brick house across the street on the northwest corner dates from 1890.

9. Edward House (401 Center Street)

Scottish immigrant Alexander Edward, an accomplished carpenter, probably borrowed the design for this house from a common pattern book. However, the hip roof, the bay which was originally three-sided, and the stone window sills indicate complexity, novelty, and willingness to play with the design. This house is historically significant because it was here in 1943 that a high-ranking LDS church leader was discovered with his mistress of thirty years, leading to his excommunication.

Turn right at the corner of 400 North and Center streets and head north along the east side of Center Street. Across the street to your left, with green porch trim, is the house of Edward's son and is now a duplex.

10. Edward House (411-413 Center Street)

Alexander Edward built this substantial Victorian Eclectic Style house for his son John in 1905. Notice the three-sided bays, shingled wall decor, concrete lintels, Tuscan columns, and Palladian windows (named after sixteenth-century Italian architect Andrea Palladio). John owned a meat market on 100 South Street. Until his father built this single-family dwelling, John and his wife lived in their father's 1903 duplex next door at 415-17 Center Street.

Farther north (past the condominiums and townhouses) almost to the corner, on your right behind the picket fence and cobblestone wall at 444 Center Street, Edward Jones, a miner, built a log house in 1873 that was later expanded by frame and adobe additions but still retains its pioneer ambiance.

Continuing north, to your left near the corner, at 445-47 Center Street, are the Belmont Terrace apartments. These were built in 1909 by Annie Pierce Bywater who supervised ZCMI's clothing manufacturing. Her second husband was city fire chief.

At the corner of 500 North (once known as Peach Street) and Center streets, to the left (southwest corner), is the renovated Cross house.

11. Cross House (467-77 Center Street)

This stuccoed adobe saltbox house was constructed about 1884 for Daniel Cross, an emigrant from Banbury, England. A plaque on the north side read "Banbury Cross," a play on the nursery rhyme. This is popularly thought to have been a polygamist house because of the two front entrances but may simply have been a duplex. Like other vernacular structures, the Cross home sits broadside to the street, has a stone foundation, simple floor plan, low roof line, and little decoration. The broken-saltbox roof slopes off in the rear like a lean-to barn.

———

☞ Side Trip. A short side trip to the right (east) up 500 North leads to the William Silver Park on your left, between Center Street and North Main. This neighborhood mini-park has benches and a slide for children. In his metal shop, Silver, a Londoner by birth and a Mormon polygamist, built the first steam engine in Utah and installed it in a boat on the Great Salt Lake. Return to the corner of 500 North and Center Street. End Side Trip.

———

Head west one-half block along 500 North Street, crossing Center

Street and Quince Street, to the building on your right (north) with the onion-shaped dome and "The Salt Lake Acting Company" above the door.

12. LDS 19th Ward House (168 West 500 North Street)

This exotic LDS chapel built in 1890 served one of the original nineteen Mormon parishes. Services were previously held at the Warm Springs Bath House on 300 West Street. The Byzantine-inspired architecture reflects the eclectic Gay Nineties when the chapel was built. Notice the Romanesque feel to the entrance. Today the church is home to the Salt Lake Acting Company and the Utah Arts Festival directors.

The gray-bricked Relief Society Hall to the west of the chapel was built in 1908. There is a social hall, erected in 1929, in the back.

Backtrack a few steps to Quince Street (158 West). Turn right, heading south. You will pass behind the Cross house and Belmont Terrace.

On your left (east), behind the cobblestone wall at 442 Quince Street, is a simple vernacular T-shaped structure built in the early 1880s and later given a fishscale gable roof and gingerbread porch. Next door (south) at 434 Quince, stonemason Robert Bowman built this sandstone and brick house in 1879 and added a polygonal domed bay in 1895. Notice the fancy brackets and ornamentation over the windows. Next door (south) is the 1907 duplex of Anna Burnswood, and two doors farther south, at 414, barely noticeable from the street but just beyond the cobblestone garage, is the 1900 Bungalow of Daniel and Marie Antoinette Lang.

Continuing south, the green ship-lap house on the right at the corner of 400 North (Plum Street) and Quince streets is the Nutting house.

13. Nutting House (160 West 400 North Street)

This simple frame Victorian house with modest gingerbread trim was built in 1894 for the Reverend John D. Nutting, pastor of the Plymouth Congregational Church, located at the time one block west. Nutting founded the Utah Gospel Mission to proselytize Mormons.

Across the street to your left, on the southeast corner of 400 North Street, is the Morrow house.

14. Morrow House (390 Quince Street)

This handsome pioneer house features some sophisticated Italianate touches—a flat roof and moulded eaves, segmented window arches, a prominent bay, and an entrance to one side rather than front-center. William Morrow built this house about 1880. Following his wife's death in 1884, the house was sold to Mormon apostle John W.

LDS 19th Ward House (III.12)

Morrow House (III.14)

Taylor, who was a plumber before entering the ministry. His father, Mormon president John Taylor, once hid here from federal authorities behind a false wall. John Taylor had fifteen wives. John W. lived in the house with one of his wives, May, whose name is inscribed in stone on the front of the house.

In 1904 Mormon apostle Reed Smoot was elected to the U.S. Senate and a senate ethics committee probed his affiliation with ongoing, secret polygamy. Church president Joseph F. Smith testified that the practice had been abolished, but Taylor and fellow apostle Matthias Cowley, against the wishes of Smith, said they would not appear before the committee and perjure themselves. In a face-saving move, they were asked to resign their church positions, and Taylor was subsequently excommunicated. Smoot retained his seat in the senate.

Next door to the south is the Carlson house.

15. Carlson House (378 Quince Street)

This house was built by August Carlson about 1885. The simple, gable-roofed structure with wood ornamentation is typical of Carpenter's Gothic Style, of which this and the Quayle house, also on Quince Street, are among the best examples in the valley. Notice the quoined wood corners and the bay window topped by a small wood balustrade with one of the ubiquitous second-story doors. Carlson was an emigrant from Sweden who became director of the State Bank of Utah, director of Zions Benefit Building Society, a University of Utah regent, and a member of the city council.

Continuing south, on your right is a Gothic frame house (375 Quince Street) with a front-center dormer, built by Danish immigrant Nils Christensen in 1887. Christensen, a harness maker, lost the house in a sheriff's sale. Three houses down on the left, on the corner of Apricot Avenue behind the cobblestone wall, is the Platts house.

16. Platts House (364 Quince Street)

The John Platts house is one of the oldest on Capitol Hill, dating from the mid-1850s. This vernacular house employs four external building materials. The cottage received an 1860s T-shaped addition. The two chimneys on the original structure recall an "I House," patterned after Indiana, Illinois, and Iowa houses which had a central passageway and a room on either side instead of a single internal wall.

With his wife Emily Price, Platts emigrated from England in 1854. He was a stonemason who also served as Brigham Young's carriage driver. He settled on the hill to raise peaches with which he paid church tithing. Difficulties over the Mormon practice of polygamy subsequently led the Plattses to disassociate themselves from the LDS church. Emily Platts became especially bitter, forbidding her children any affiliation with Mormons. National Register of Historic Places.

Platts House (III.16)

Passing Apricot Avenue, notice on the right (west) the Carpenter's Gothic Quayle house.

17. Quayle House (355 Quince Street)

This quaint frame house with wood gingerbread trim was built as a rental property between 1884-89 by Thomas Quayle. Quayle was born on the Isle of Man in 1835, immigrated to the United States with his family in 1840, and traveled to Utah in 1847. Thomas and his brother ran away to the California gold fields as teenagers, where they began freighting supplies from Sacramento to mining camps. They later returned to Utah to establish a freighting company, including a stint carrying gold for Wells Fargo Company. In 1975 the house was moved from its original location at Growers' Market, about 400 South and West Temple streets, to make way for the new Hilton Hotel. Until 1995 it served as headquarters for the Utah Heritage Foundation (now housed in the Memory Grove Memorial House) which oversees preservation of historic sites.

☞ **Side Trip.** Continue south to the house on your right (west) at 335 Quince Street, built by English immigrant James Watson, the stonemason who built the Eagle Emporium. He was later Salt Lake City mayor. The house is a vernacular T-shaped structure, built about 1870. His brother and business partner, Joseph, lived across the street at 334 Quince.

Next door at 331-33 Quince Street is the Matthew Asper house, built in 1908. His brother William's brick house with intricate woodwork is next door at 325 Quince Street, built about 1885. William was a skilled carpenter who is credited with the impressive circular staircase in the Assembly Hall. Notice the weather vane.

Across the street to the left (east), three houses down at 314 Quince, is one of the oldest houses in the district—a stucco-over-adobe house built in the mid-1860s by Richard Morris, a Welsh immigrant. The porch was added later. Morris was president of the Utah Soap Factory, which was located a block west of the 19th Ward chapel. Notice the non-functional second-story door. National Register of Historic Places.

Backtrack to Apricot Avenue. **End Side Trip.**

Climb Apricot Avenue east. Notice the snow and water drain which bisects the middle of the street. Across the street to your left (north) is the Victorian Batley cottage.

18. Batley House (144 Apricot Avenue)

Louie Platts Batley moved into her T-shaped house in 1892. Later she met a barber whom she married and bore two children. It is thought that she copied the architectural design for her house from a pattern book. At least four other Carpenter's Gothic homes in the Marmalade District share this design.

On your right (south), at 135 Apricot Avenue, covered with vines, is the 1905 cottage of Albert Adkison, a real estate entrepreneur.

Continue east to the corner of Almond and Apricot streets and turn right onto Almond, heading south. The 1-story Victorian Eclectic house on your left at 350 Almond Street, with the polygonal bay window, was built in 1884 by James Fowler, a marble cutter. Many Marmalade home owners were skilled laborers.

Two houses south at 328 Almond Street, across from the neighborhood parking lot, was shoemaker Richard Collett's T-shaped cottage.

Two houses farther south on the east side, set back from the street and partially concealed by trees—with the street number posted on the most prominent tree—is the Rawlings house.

19. Rawlings House (322 Almond Street)

Tucked away on Almond Street, this charming cottage was built for cabinet maker Edwin Rawlings in 1873. Rawlings played in the martial band for the local militia. He housed two wives and five children in this little home until 1910, when he built a 2-story duplex next door at 318 Almond Street.

Across the street to the west at 321 Almond Street, Thomas Jenkins, an Australian carpenter who moonlighted as a mine shaft framer, built this 1901 pattern-book house for himself and, a few feet to the rear, a similar structure for his friend Ebenezer Beesley, Jr., a shoe finisher whose father lived at the end of the street on the corner. Joseph Shaw, a horse groomer, built the 1-story brick house farther south at 309 Almond Street (the garage came later).

On the northeast corner of 300 North and Almond streets is the Beesley house.

20. Beesley House (80 West 300 North Street)

This T-shaped stuccoed adobe manor was built in the early 1870s for Ebenezer Beesley, violinist and conductor of the Mormon Tabernacle Choir and Salt Lake Theatre Orchestra. He also founded the Beesley Music Company. Notice in the front that Beesley's house features another superfluous second-story door leading to a superficial portico. A polygamist, Beesley had sixteen children. He was a handcart pioneer who supported himself initially as a shoemaker. National Register of Historic Places.

Turn right on 300 North Street (once called Currant Street), walk a few steps west, and cross to the south to pick up Almond Street where it skirts the edge of the hill. From here, looking to the west, you can see

West High School, with the airport in the distance, and beyond that Antelope Island in the middle of Great Salt Lake. You can also see an old water tower, the Triad Center, the Delta Center, and Doubletree Hotel—with the Oquirrh Mountains rounding out the view.

As you head south the street curves to the left and you can see the LDS temple with the Key Bank and Kennecott buildings behind it. Eventually you will see the Eagle Gate Tower and the LDS church office highrise.

On your left are the Capitol Hill apartments, a row of town house condominiums, and the rear sides of Trevi Towers and Zion Summit condominium complexes. On your right (west), at 217-19 Almond, is the 1893 brick Victorian house of Welsh immigrant William Jones, a plasterer.

At the end of Almond Street, turn left and walk along the railed sidewalk east. Across 200 North Street to your right is the Deseret Gymnasium, completed in 1965 by the LDS church and expanded ten years later. This stretch of 200 North Street is where document forger Mark Hofmann parked his car in 1985 and accidentally detonated a homemade pipe bomb.

Continue east to the corner of North Main and 200 North streets where you will see the McCune mansion on the northeast corner. Cross North Main Street to the east, using the marked pedestrian crosswalks.

21. Alfred McCune Mansion (200 North Main Street)

This magnificent 3-story, 21-room Shingle Style house was designed by S. C. Dallas and completed in 1901. It was the first $1-million house in Utah. McCune was born in Calcutta, India, which is reflected in the distinctive Asian flair to the mansion, although the house is a replica of an estate McCune encountered on Riverside Drive in New York City. The interior includes liberal use of imported materials such as Russian mahogany.

At age twenty-one McCune contracted to build portions of the Utah Southern Railroad, becoming one of the largest railroad contractors in the Rocky Mountain region. He also purchased the city trolleys. He then became partner with J. P. Morgan, William Hearst, and F. Vanderbilt in the Peruvian Cero de Pasco mines.

For years the house was home to the McCune School of Music and Art, run by faculty from the defunct LDS University. The mansion is now a social center used for receptions and seminars. Besides the prominent conical turret and oval portico, note the tile shingles on the third story, the rusticated lower levels, and wrought-iron ornaments. National Register of Historic Places.

――――

☞ **Side Trip.** Walk east along 200 North Street past the McCune mansion to the stuccoed adobe house across the street (south) at 36 East, built about 1880 by Mormon leader J. Golden Kimball, son of Apostle Heber Kimball. Golden is remembered for his earthy metaphors and "colorful" language, reflecting his occupation as a mule skinner before his call to the ministry.

A little farther east, on your left at 45 East, is the spacious Italianate Seckels house. Louis Seckels and wife Sarah, daughter of Heber Kimball, built this edifice in 1889. The windows, designed for a view of the Salt Lake temple, were set behind twelve columns which represent the twelve Mormon apostles.

Next door to the east is the Crismon house (53 East), with the distinctive gambrel roof, built in 1905 for Charles Crismon, a mineral assayer. Crismon's father imported the first honey bees to Utah from California.

Return to the McCune mansion at the corner of Main Street. **End Side Trip.**

———

At 200 North and Main streets, proceed south on North Main to Gordon Place Alley (155 North), passing the 1906 classically detailed Kensington Apartments and the newer Deseret Apartments on your left.

Turn left (east) at the mid-block boulder sign marked "Kimball-Whitney Cemetery," passing along the north side of the Kimball Apartments to the park entrance. Proceed to the small cemetery inside the park on the left (north).

22. Kimball Cemetery (41 Gordon Place)

Heber Kimball, counselor to LDS church president Brigham Young, was one of the original pioneer settlers of the Salt Lake Valley. He had forty-three wives. He died in 1868 a few weeks after being thrown from a buggy. Newell Whitney, presiding bishop of the Mormon church, was also buried here.

Continue east along the brick walkway through Gordon Place Park to State Street. The second house on your right (south) as you emerge from the park is the Dougall house.

23. Dougall House (145 North State Street)

Constructed about 1904, this Victorian Eclectic abode is noted for its classical details such as doric columns, exterior wood trim, and swan neck pediment on the dormer window. The owner, William Dougall, was grandson of Brigham Young, manager of the Deseret Telegraph Company, and an insurance agent.

Backtrack a few steps and proceed north along State Street. Across to your right (east) is the Snow house.

24. Snow House (158 North State Street)

The horizontal lines, broad eaves, brown brick, deep porch, and high brick-to-stucco transition on the Ashby Snow house, built in 1909, are typical elements of Prairie School architecture. Ashby was son of Mormon pioneer Erastus Snow and associated with Utah Portland Cement, Hotel Utah, Utah and Idaho Sugar (U & I), Saltair, and other ventures.

Next door, north of the Snow house, is the Gallacher house.

25. Gallacher House (170 North State Street)

This red brick Elizabethan Revival house was completed in 1925. Notice how the raised masses, ornamental timbers, and sloping roof over the entrance create a picturesque effect. Edwin Gallacher, a retired U.S. army sergeant, married Ashby Snow's daughter and was associated with Utah Portland Cement and Saltair.

Next door on the corner (southeast corner of 200 North and State streets) is another, more spacious example of Elizabethan style.

26. Cannon House (180 North State Street)

Willard Cannon, son of Mormon leader George Cannon and president of U & I Sugar, erected this home in 1918. Elizabethan and Tudor styles began as a cost-saving device, using fewer timbers (called half timbering) and filling the spaces between with sticks and mud covered with stucco. It evolved into high chic. Notice the arched entrance, wood casement windows, and asphalt shingles simulating a thatched roof. The tall chimney adds to the picturesque look.

To your left, back on this west side of the street, is the Hall house.

27. Hall House (169 North State Street)

Lucius Hall was manager of the Salt Lake Sewing Machine Company. When he built this Box Style house in 1906, he included a 2-story porch with a wrought-iron spiral staircase connecting the ground and second floor levels.

Next door to the north, on the southwest corner, is Hall's earlier 1884 Federal house, with some Georgian trappings. The original walls were bricked over in the 1940s. Notice the rooftop widow's walk.

Across 200 North, diagonally to your right on the northeast corner, is the Brooks house.

28. Brooks House (204 North State Street)

Built in 1890, this large, atypical Victorian Queen Anne house sits high above the street with its imposing 3-story candle-snuffer turret and third-story balcony. In the 1890s Queen Anne extravagance became a sign of success. The departure from Federal symmetry and simplicity was only one manifestation of excess in this decade. Among other things, architects experimented with a variety of building materials and rich, varied colors, most notably the wood-shingled, patterned walls.

A county surveyor, Charles Brooks supplemented his income by free-lancing for mining companies. His wife Millicent was a daughter of William Godbe who opposed Brigham Young's prohibition on mining (which Young felt was speculative and frivolous). In 1897 the Brookses sold their house to U.S. marshall Glen Miller and his wife Libbie. The house has since been converted to apartments.

Cross 200 North Street to the Woodruff mansion on the northwest corner.

29. Woodruff Mansion (225 North State Street)

Edward Woodruff built this Second Renaissance Revival palace in 1906. Notice the rusticated ground floor, arched entrance, columns, tile roof, wide eaves with flower blossoms in relief, intricate molding, and wrought iron. The interior was equally impressive, with stained glass windows, mahogany paneling, and leather-covered walls. Woodruff was a physician with the Union Pacific Railroad. Franklin Riter, Woodruff's son-in-law, inherited the house. He served as head of the European office of the Judge Advocate for the U.S. Army during World War II. National Register of Historic Places.

Continue north to the matching carriage house at the rear of the mansion. Across State Street, next door to the Brooks Queen Anne, is the Victorian Eclectic house of Lulu Smith.

30. Smith House (208 North State Street)

Lulu Smith owned the Lace House Dress Shop. She later lost her house over a dispute with neighbor Libbie Miller and was forced to sell to Fred Stauffer, a physician and former mayor of Eureka, Utah. Notice how her brick house rises high above the street line.

North of Smith's house, behind the stone retaining wall, notice the two 1890s alcoves at 210 and 214 North State Street, partially concealed by trees. They share a flight of sandstone stairs, branching out midway from the street. George Ellerbeck, a physician, built the home to the south with a veranda and cross gables, and Murray Godbe, a pharmacist and son of William Godbe, built the house at the northern end of the stairs. The Godbe house was designed by Richard Kletting who also designed the state capitol and the Saltair resort on the Great Salt Lake.

Heading north to Hillside Avenue (240 North), turn right and walk east one block, past the Mediterranean Style "Hillside Court" on your right at number 114, to the corner of East Capitol Street (120 East). Here you have a side view of the Dickson house across the street to your left (north).

31. Dickson House (273 East Capitol Street)

This Georgian Revival manor was constructed in 1905 for William Dickson, U.S. district attorney for the territory of Utah and member of

Woodruff Mansion (III.29)

the non-Mormon Liberal Party. Notice the fanlight windows, keystones, and tall chimneys. In the front is an imposing entrance with heavy 2-story columns and elaborate molding. A northern addition did not replicate the detail.

Turn right, heading south on East Capitol Street, passing an International Style house and a Colonial Revival house on the right, to the staircase mid-block on the left (east), near the lamp post, bordered by a low cement wall on either side.

Descend the stairs to Fourth Avenue, continue east to the corner of Canyon Road (130 East), and turn left, heading north to the second house from the northwest corner.

32. Anderson House (207 Canyon Road)

The wood trim of this otherwise simple house shows the builder's interest in Eastlake detail. The designer and owner was Danish architect Herman Anderson. It was completed in 1890, but Anderson died here of tuberculosis at age thirty-five, leaving behind a wife and ten children.

Proceed next door to the north.

33. Kimball House (211 Canyon Road)

This small 1904 brick cottage with fish-scale shingling and rusticated stone lintels housed Elliot Kimball, a Union Pacific brakeman, and family. Kimball served in the First Volunteer Cavalry during the Spanish-American War. Notice the rock window sills, stained glass transoms, and elliptical window portal on the bay.

Next door, nearly concealed by trees, is the Snow house.

34. Snow House (217 Canyon Road)

Erastus Snow built this 2-story, L-shaped, stuccoed adobe dwelling for his polygamous wife Minerva. Erastus was a member of the first pioneer company into the valley and an LDS apostle. Notice the heavy wood lintel, bracketed front bay window, decorative wood trim, and quarter-round windows in the gables. Reportedly the house was designed by Truman Angell, architect for the LDS temple.

The brick building with the prominent cupola farther up the street on your left is Ottinger Hall.

35. Ottinger Hall (233 Canyon Road)

Ottinger Hall was constructed in 1900 by the Volunteer Firemen's Association as a clubhouse, library, and museum. The museum still contains fire department relics and memorabilia, a book collection, and paintings by artist and volunteer fire chief George Ottinger. The museum is open only for pre-arranged tours.

Notice how the building's simple, rectangular plan is enlivened by the variation in the roof line, segmented brick windows, and central arched entrance. When the hall was constructed, the city had six volunteer companies, most of which worked exclusively with buckets, hooks,

Ottinger Hall (III.35)

and ladders. Three companies had hand pumps and one had a steam engine. A few miles of water mains had been installed which drew from a water tank near Ottinger Hall, but the water pressure was unpredictable. National Register of Historic Places.

Continue north to see the modest Second Empire Pratt home to your right.

36. Pratt House (252 Canyon Road)

Helaman Pratt's 1880 home was one of the first in the canyon, which is why it faces the city instead of the road. Generally, French Second Empire is more pretentious, but this eclectic house does have a mansard roof—sitting like a lid on a storage box—embellished by a wide frieze with brackets. Notice also the dormers and curious arched window bays.

Continue north to Memory Grove. The bronze plaques on the rock lamp pillars at the entrance feature in relief romanticized portrayals of war widows.

37. Memory Grove Park

Establishment of this 20-acre park memorializing Utah's veterans was primarily the work of the Salt Lake City chapter of the Service Star Legion. Dedicated in 1924, Memory Grove sits today on what was originally a flour mill site, then gravel pit and neighborhood dump. Canyon Road, which traverses the grove, is now a popular walking, jogging, and bicycling area leading to City Creek Canyon and the mountains to the northeast.

Enter the park and follow the stone path. The hill to your right (east) is called Friendship Hill; the hill to your left (west) is Gold Star Hill; and the pond in front of you to the right is known as Harbor Lake. Throughout the park red flowers were intended to represent sacrifice, blue flowers loyalty, white flowers peace. Ivy starts from the graves of George Washington and Robert E. Lee were used in the landscaping. A sprinkling system was installed after the first 300 newly planted trees died.

Turn right just before the pond and proceed east to the gazebo behind the flagpole, a memorial to World War I martyrs. To the right of the gazebo is a French *merci* box car which distributed gifts to U.S. cities following World War II. Left of the gazebo is a Vietnam-era armored vehicle which highlights the park's theme as a memorial to soldiers.

Follow the path on the east side of the park past the German field gun to the Meditation Chapel northeast of the bridge. The Meditation Chapel was built at a cost of $100,000 and dedicated in 1948. It is constructed of reinforced concrete with exterior walls of pink Georgian marble and interior walls of Italian Botticcino marble. The floor is a mosaic of French and Italian marbles. The ceiling is of cast plaster, the roof of sheet copper. Exterior light enters the chapel through four stained glass windows representing the four branches of the armed services. It is intended for meditation and prayer and is devoid of overt religious symbolism.

Continue north past the "For God and Country" 145th Field Artillery monument to the cobblestone bridge. Cross the bridge and street west to the French Provincial Style Memorial House and rest rooms north of the house. This structure was built in 1904, originally as a barn, tool house, and blacksmith shop. It was remodeled and rededicated as the Memorial House in 1926. Since 1995 it has housed the Utah Heritage Foundation and can be leased as a reception center.

Head south to the full-scale Liberty Bell replica on your left—one of 100 replicas cast by the original maker. Continue south a few steps to the Rotary Club stairs on your right (west). Climb the stairs through Horizon Grove (with discretion at night) and follow the path to the top. The pathway forks a number of times, but any direction takes you to East Capitol Boulevard. When you emerge at the top, carefully cross the street to the cement path leading to the rear of the tall, rough-hewn rock monument with nineteenth-century soldiers portrayed in bas-relief and in bronze.

38. Mormon Battalion Monument (Capitol Hill)

In memory of 500 Mormons who enlisted for the United States in the Mexican War of 1846, sculptor Gilbert Riswold created this 1927 monument. The battalion served a six-month tour of duty between Coucil Bluffs, Iowa, and San Diego. As well as raising much-needed currency for immigration, these volunteers seemed to reaffirm patriotism at a time when it was in question. Many lingered in California and played a role in the discovery of gold at Sutter's Mill.

Turn left (south) and cross 300 North Street at the crosswalk back to the Old City Hall. To the east, on the corner, is the White Memorial Chapel, built in 1881.

39. White Memorial Chapel (150 East 300 North Street)

Originally situated farther down the hill, the LDS 18th Ward chapel was among the first in the valley to feature a steeple, reflecting the New England ancestry of Utah's early immigrants. The chapel was dismantled in 1973 and reconstructed at its present location seven years later with new brick. The doors, pews, pulpit, and stained glass windows are preserved. Now owned by the state, the chapel is available for non-denominational community functions. It is open only by appointment.

Looking back across 300 North Street, in the foreground of the Mormon Battalion monument, notice the "date garden," where the plantings change daily to show day and month.

This ends the Capitol Hill and City Creek Canyon tour.

IV.
The Avenues and
South Temple Street

DISTANCE: 4.5 MILES   TIME: 5 HOURS

In 1976 South Temple Street became Utah's first state historic district. In the nineteenth century it was known colloquially as Brigham Street. Not long after the street's most celebrated resident, Brigham Young, began work on his spectacular Gardo House, other mansions appeared along this stately 72-foot-wide boulevard. The street is lined primarily with large, high-style residences built from the late 1880s through 1915, as well as some modern commercial buildings.

The area north of South Temple Street is known as the Avenues. Originally named after shade trees, north-south running streets were renamed in 1885 after the letters of the alphabet, while east-west running streets were identified with numbers. The area consists of small blocks, about half the size of most 660-foot-square city blocks, making this tour half as long as it may appear on the map. An historic upper-middle class neighborhood built on an inclining bench, the Avenues is characterized by small-, medium-, and large-sized residences from the Victorian and Bungalow era, as well as a few small vernacular houses from the earlier Mormon pioneer period.

Please note that addresses on South Temple Street do not harmonize with addresses in the Avenues. For instance, the street signs for Q Street change from 1100 East to 1000 East between South Temple Street and First Avenue without a bend in the road. The Avenues were laid out separately and never numerically integrated into the rest of the city.

Parking is most easily available on the street north of 2nd Avenue between B and C streets.

1. Catholic Cathedral of the Madeleine (331 East South Temple Street)

The exterior of this Romanesque sandstone masterpiece took ten years to build, 1899-1909, and the interior was completed seventeen years later in 1926. It was through the efforts of Bishop Lawrence Scanlan, an Irish immigrant educated at All Hallows College in Dublin, and prominent parishioners who made their fortunes in mining, that this dream became a reality. The body of Bishop Scanlan lies under the altar; a bronze plaque memorializes him at the foot of the cathedral steps. Be sure to notice the bat gargoyles on the exterior. The cathedral was designed by Carl Neuhausen.

Wall Mansion (IV.3)

Entering the cathedral, just past the entrance to the nave is the baptistry which allows proselytes the option of baptism by immersion. Notice the intricate woodwork throughout the interior, such as the carved angels atop the confessionals. The magnificent stained glass windows were made in Munich, and the recent $10-million renovation restored the original brilliance of the frescoes, painted columns, and colorful vaulted ceiling ribs. Behind the marble altar and ornate tabernacle, on the apse wall to the right of the crucified Jesus, is a judgment mural by Felix Lieftuchter. Among the figures portrayed are Salome carrying John the Baptist's head and a 6-toed Eve evidencing her fallen state. Open daily 8:00 a.m.-5:30 p.m.; tours 1:00 p.m. National Register of Historic Places.

Back outside, proceed east on South Temple Street, past the cathedral rectory, and cross C Street.

2. First Presbyterian Church (357 East South Temple Street)

Built in 1906, this Scottish-influenced Gothic Revival church is noted for its red sandstone exterior, quarried from Red Butte Canyon, its prominent rectangular tower, and stained glass windows. It was designed after the medieval cathedral at Carlisle, complete with crenelated bastions. It has an artesian well in the basement. Construction was overseen by noted Utah architect Walter Ware. The church is open for services only, Sundays 9:00 a.m. and 11:00 a.m.

Next door is the Wall mansion, now part of the campus of the LDS Business College.

3. Wall Mansion (411 East South Temple Street)

Enos Wall, a mining magnate who helped develop an ore reduction process at the Bingham Copper Mine, was non-Mormon and opposed to polygamy. As a Mason and president of the Alta Club, he saw to it that Mormons were excluded from these institutions. Ironically, his mansion now houses a Mormon college.

Designed by Richard Kletting and constructed in 1905 around an existing brick house built by Mormon Abraham Smoot, Wall's $300,000 renaissance villa contained fireplaces in all six bedrooms, a ballroom on the third floor, and a rooftop promenade. Unnoticeable behind the veneer is reinforced concrete—the first residence in Utah to use this medium. Wall's mansion was sold to the Jewish Community Center in 1926, resold in 1950 to an insurance agency, and finally purchased by the LDS church in 1961. Other buildings were added to the property in 1962 when it became LDS Business College, although these early school administrators chose not to continue the classical motifs of columns, scrolled braces, decorative keystones, and wrought-iron railings. Through the efforts of a recent president, the mansion itself has been restored. Open to the public.

Walk along the east side of the mansion to the far corner of the student services building (on the right), turn right and proceed east

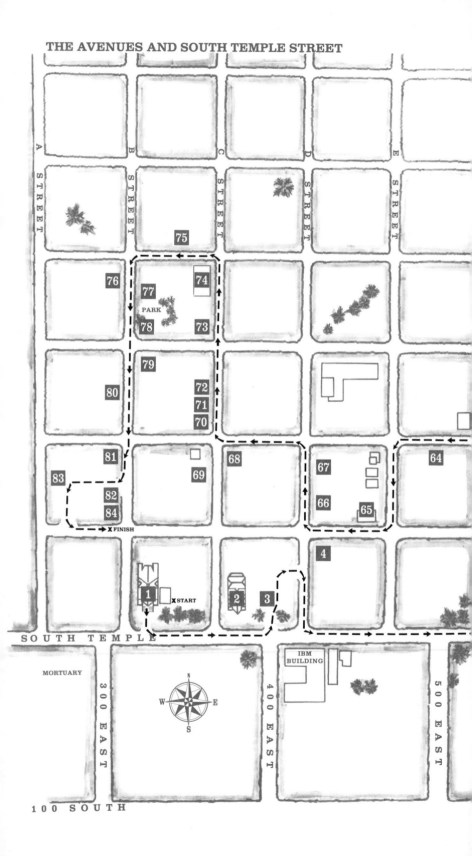

THE AVENUES AND SOUTH TEMPLE STREET

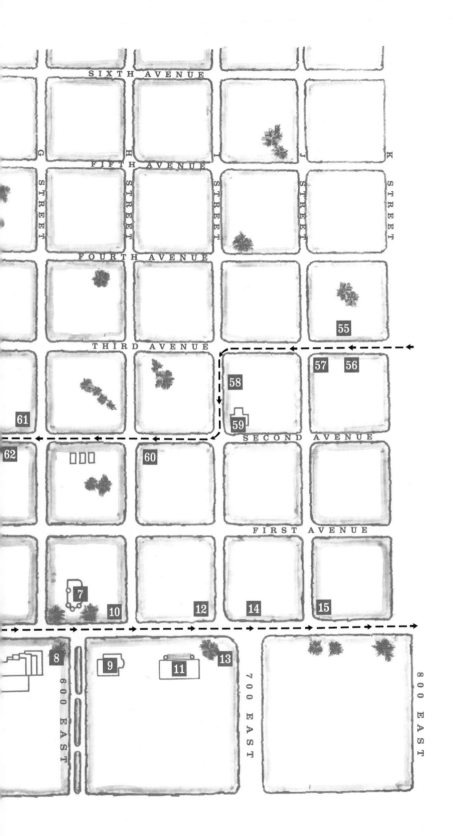

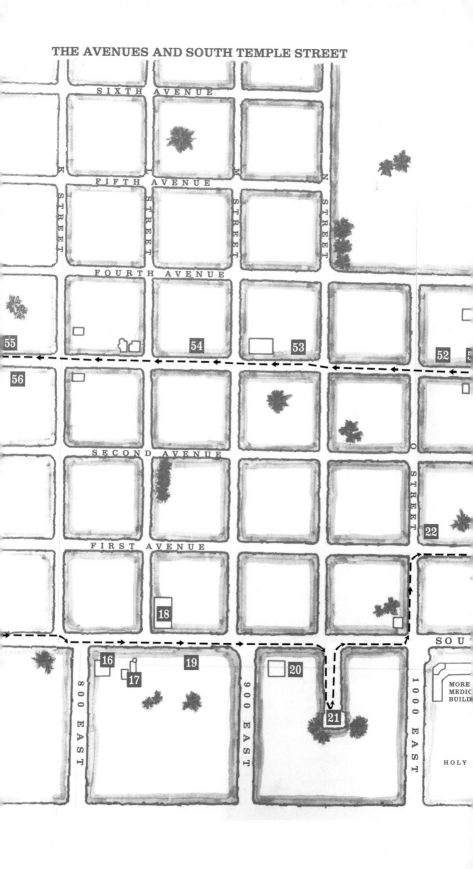

SALT LAKE CITY CEMETERY

ENTRANCE

THIRD AVENUE

49

45

48 47 46

44

41 40

39

24

26

43 42

38

25

27

30 31

32 33

34

35

37

36

28 29

1100 EAST

1200 EAST

1300 EAST

MPLE

ITAL

Q STREET

R STREET

S STREET

T STREET

U STREET

along the walkway to D Street. From here you can see the Daynes house on the southeast corner of First Avenue across the street to the left.

4. Daynes House (38 D Street)

This Box Style (cube-shaped) house was completed in 1904 for Joseph Daynes, Salt Lake Tabernacle organist. He started his thirty-three-year tenure in that position at the age of sixteen. Notice the front-center dormer, off-center entrance, stone foundation, and modest portico which are typical of Box Style houses.

Return to South Temple Street, turn left and proceed east. Across the street to your right (south) is the glass-and-cement IBM building, followed by the 1910 workshop of inventor Alfred Whitmore at 430 East South Temple Street, where he assembled electric cars. Whitmore later began the first commercial production of oxygen in Utah. Next door, Mrs. Backer's Pastry Shop (434 East) has been in business since 1926.

On your left (north) is the Ritz apartment complex at 435 East South Temple Street, built in 1925.

Cross E Street and continue east to the far corner of F Street to one of the most lavish Brigham Street mansions.

5. Keith Mansion (529 East South Temple Street)

This Neo-Classical Revival limestone masterpiece recalls a Greek temple with its central block and symmetrical wings, massive columns supporting a broad pediment, double portico, and stone foundation and balustrades. Notice also the etched window transoms and wrought iron doors. This showpiece was designed by Frederick Hale and built in 1900 for David Keith, an immigrant from Nova Scotia, who was partner with Thomas Kearns in Park City's Silver King mine.

The interior is equally impressive, despite a 1986 fire which destroyed the upper two floors. The original cathedral-like octagonal rotunda and skylight have been expertly replicated. Originally, the butler's pantry was equipped with a warming table through which hot water circulated. A walk-in refrigerator was cooled by one ton of ice. In the laundry, wet clothes were hung in a closet through which hot air circulated.

At the street curb in front of the mansion are well-preserved stone carriage steps and a horse hitch. Similar disembarking platforms and tethers can be found in front of other Brigham Street manors.

A grand carriage house to the east, set back from the street behind an entrance bracketed by stone bowl-shaped planters, was built to include a bowling alley, shooting gallery, and servants' quarters.

While Keith and Kearns were employed by the Woodside Mine in Park City, they noticed that the vein of ore extended to a neighboring property, which they purchased and developed on their own. Not as successful in his personal life as in business, Keith's first wife reportedly left him for another man, and his youngest daughter bore his adopted

Keith Mansion (IV.5)

son's child. For the rest of her life she wore a heavy black veil and rarely left the house, eventually committing suicide.

The house was bought in 1914 by Mayor Ezra Thompson, and later renovated by Terracor land developers. It now houses Leucadia Financial Corporation.

Proceed east next door.

6. Hall House (551 East South Temple Street)

This is where territorial secretary William Hall established his residence in 1898. Hall was a Kentucky Confederate who fought for the South during the Civil War and was later assigned to Utah by U.S. president Grover Cleveland. Hall's house features an octagonal corner bay with a conical dome, shingling above the first level, a curved, columned porch, and wide bracketed cornices characteristic of Queen Anne Style.

Continue east on South Temple Street, noticing the upscale concrete and glass Governor's Plaza condominiums across the street to your right (south). Cross G Street east to the Kearns mansion—the crown jewel of Brigham Street, which had been the governor's official residence from 1937 to December 1993, when a fire destroyed much of the interior.

7. Kearns Mansion (603 East South Temple Street)

This French-inspired Chateauesque mansion was designed by Carl Neuhausen and built in 1902 with a limestone exterior and exotic imported wood interior. Chateauesque prevailed among the wealthy during the gilded age of "robber barons," beginning with William Vanderbilt. Highlights include the 3-story, round, corner towers, the front portico supported by marble columns, rounded dormers, and oolitic chimneys. On the south side notice the balcony colonnade and rococo window trim. On the east side, two relief images of Atlas appear to support the weight of the cornice. The house was used in 1972 to film the television movie, *House of the Seven Corpses.*

Inside, the front reception hall boasts a mosaic floor of hand-cut marble. The library contrasts black oak with red marble, and the dining room exhibits mahogany walls and ceiling. A multi-headed shower closet and vaults for jewels, silver, and wine were among the interior amenities. Reportedly, a ton of coal was required daily in the winter for heat. National Register of Historic Places.

Be sure to notice the carriage house to the northeast. The entrance sports a worn horse's head relief which Kearns's sons are said to have used for target practice with slingshots.

Thomas Kearns immigrated from Canada and married his partner John Judge's niece. Kearns's wife and children lived several years in Switzerland after a kidnapping threat. In 1903 Theodore Roosevelt—whom Kearns resembled in appearance—commented to a friend that the guest list at Kearns's home included a Catholic bishop and a Mormon polygamist apostle. In addition to Kearns's mining fortune, he

Kearns Mansion (IV.7)

Kearns Mansion, detail (IV.7)

Kearns Mansion (IV.7)

served as a U.S. senator and publisher of the *Salt Lake Tribune*. In 1918 he was fatally hit by a car on Main Street. Kearns's son, Thomas Jr., founded Utah's chapter of Alcoholics Anonymous.

Before you continue east, look back across the street directly opposite the Kearns mansion to see the Gentsch house on the southwest corner of 600 East and South Temple Street.

8. Gentsch House (576 East South Temple Street)

This Queen Anne house boasts slanted and square bay windows, ornamental ironwork, and leaded stained glass windows. Frederick Gentsch, an agent for Pacific Express Company, built the house in 1889.

Mayor Ezra Thompson purchased the house in 1898 and lived here thirty years. Thompson began working at age seventeen driving a 4-yoke team of oxen between North Platte, Nebraska, and Salt Lake City. He was elected mayor in 1898 and re-elected twice but forced to resign in 1907 when implicated in a rigged gambling scam. The house was later headquarters for the Children's Service Society.

Just east of the Gentsch house, across 600 East Street on the southeast corner, you can see the Second Renaissance Revival Walker mansion.

9. Walker Mansion (610 East South Temple Street)

This mansion was built in 1904 for Matthew Walker, co-founder of Walker Bank. Walker and his brothers sympathized with the Godbeites, Mormon dissenters to Brigham Young's boycott of gentile merchants, and were excommunicated. Young afterwards gave encouragement to anyone he thought would dilute the Walkers' influence.

Notice the mansion's red tile roof, arched colonnade, cream-colored stucco exterior, and broad balcony. In the foyer Walker had an Aeolian organ with pipes extending to the third floor, where a Tiffany skylight and chandelier graced the ceiling. Other luxuries included a wine cellar, bowling alley, and stable. The architect was Frederick Hale, who also designed the Keith mansion.

Again on the north side of South Temple Street, east of the Kearns mansion, is the Glendenning residence.

10. Glendenning House (617 East South Temple Street)

This transitional Victorian structure includes Georgian Revival elements such as the keystones and flat-arched windows. The downstairs hallway features a decorative parquet floor. It was built in 1885 for James Glendenning, mayor of Salt Lake City and co-founder of the Chamber of Commerce. It currently houses the Utah Arts Council.

Continue east across H Street. You can see the imposing columns and guardian sphinxes of the Masonic Temple across South Temple Street to your right (south).

Walker Mansion (IV.9)

11. Masonic Temple (650 East South Temple Street)

The architectural style—evident in the massive rectangular form, the pair of sphinxes at the entrance, the papyrus blossom columns, rope molding, and winged solar disk of Horus—is Egyptian Revival. Even the flagpole bases bear papyriform embellishment. Also notice the Masonic compass and square in the frieze. To the right of the entrance, behind papyrus blossom vases, a ramp leads to a small door with Horus and scarab reliefs through which caskets are passed after funerals. The interior includes a 1,400-seat auditorium, an Aztec banquet hall, and fraternal lodge rooms in Gothic, Egyptian, Moorish, and American Colonial styles. The building was completed in 1926.

Continue east. To your left, at the corner of I Street, is the Fife house.

12. Fife House (667 East South Temple Street)

This high-contrast Georgian Revival house was built in 1916 for William Fife, founder of a men's clothing store. Notice the stone quoins at the corner and the round portico over the center entrance. Fife later became director of Continental Bank and Trust Company. Like most other property in the Avenues, this originally belonged to Brigham Young and was valuable because of the wells located here.

Cross I Street. From here you can see the Kahn house across the street on the southwest corner of 700 East and South Temple streets.

13. Kahn House (678 East South Temple Street)

This 2.5-story brick Victorian Queen Anne with rusticated stone trim was built in 1889. It is known for its fancy woodwork on the porches and roof crest and for the corner turret lined with small dormers (added later), topped by a finial. Because the decorative polygonal turret faces the intersection, it is a favorite local landmark. Emmanuel Kahn, a Prussian immigrant, owned a downtown shop that sold "groceries, cigars, and tobacco." Kahn was a founder of Congregation B'Nai Israel, helped organize the Liberal Party, and supported the Young Men's Literary Association. National Register of Historic Places.

Continuing east, the second structure to your left (north) is the Evans house.

14. Evans House (701 East South Temple Street)

This ivy-covered English Tudor Revival house, with a water tank in the attic for indoor flushing toilets, was built in 1911 for Morris Evans. The house has two marble bathrooms. More distinctive, however, is the decorative half-timbering of the broad-gabled façade. Evans made his fortune in cattle and coal, but his passion was sports. He owned a sporting goods store, sponsored bicycle races, and helped underwrite the Salt Lake Bees, the city's first baseball team in the Pacific Coast League. The Bees moved to California to become the Hollywood Stars in 1925 but returned in 1958 to be managed by Enid Cosgriff, the country's first female manager.

Continue east across J Street to the cream-colored brick corner house on your left.

15. Jackling House (731 East South Temple Street)

This surprisingly modest Colonial Revival house, designed by Walter Ware and built in 1898 for William Sherman, was acquired in 1904 by Daniel Jackling, one of the wealthiest men in the state. The house was reportedly acquired for his mistress. The "Copper Prince," as Jackling was known, became a multi-millionaire developing Bingham Canyon after Enos Wall, discoverer, was unable to extract the mineral from low-grade ore. A graduate of Missouri School of Mines, Jackling invented a successful separation process (making a life-long enemy of Wall). Today Jackling's statue stands in the state capitol rotunda.

Jackling was Utah's most famous playboy. He reportedly courted several life-long lovers, financed a Commercial Street brothel, and hosted extravagant parties on his private railroad cars and luxury yacht. Jackling divided his evenings between this house and Hotel Utah, which he helped fund. He later moved to San Francisco, where he occupied the Mark Hopkins penthouse.

Continue east, across K Street, turn right and traverse South Temple Street to the south. The Victorian mansion of "Sheep Queen" Elizabeth Bonnemort once stood on this (southwest) corner. Not only was she one of the wealthiest sheep ranchers in the country, she was a prominent organizer in the National Wool Growers Association. Turn left (east) across 800 East to the Downey house.

16. Downey House (808 East South Temple Street)

This striking Shingle Style house is an architectural relative of the Queen Anne, distinguished by its shingle wall surface and subdivision of wall surfaces. Although the bell-shaped tower with the knobbed finial is juxtaposed by a plain brick chimney, stone lintels, and fan lights, these do not offset the overall heaviness. The house was built in 1893 for Major George Downey who served with the U.S. army at Gettysburg. He became president of Commercial National Bank and later vice president of Rocky Mountain Bell Telephone Company. There is a compatible carriage house to the east. The architect, Frederick Hale, also designed the Keith and Walker mansions.

Proceed east to the 2.5-story turreted Shingle Style Parker house.

17. Parker House (824 East South Temple Street)

Frank Parker's architect succeeded in focusing attention on the classical motifs of the entrance rather than the Victorian tower. The shingled house was built in 1901 by the owner of the Parker Lumber Company.

Across the street to the left (north) are the Neo-Classical Maryland apartments (now condominiums).

18. Maryland (839 East South Temple Street)

The Maryland apartment complex was built in 1912 by architect Bernard Mecklenburg and named after him. After being interned during World War I because of his German ancestry, Mecklenburg changed his apartments' name to Maryland. Servants' quarters in the basement were equipped with electric bells for summoning. Notice the marble steps and the large curved balcony brackets.

East of the Parke house is the Ladies' Literary Club.

19. Ladies' Literary Club (850 East South Temple Street)

This early-modern period Prairie clubhouse was designed by the tempestuous team of local architects Walter Ware and Albert Treganza and built in 1912 for one of the oldest women's clubs in the nation. Ware was a business-oriented designer, eager to please clients. Treganza was volatile and experimental. Their competing personalities were thought to have complemented each other.

Notice the horizontal lines, full-length porch, and brick to the second-level window sills. Inside, a reception and drawing room lead to a 2-storied auditorium which seats 350. National Register of Historic Places.

Continue east to the corner, passing what were once the Mary-Beth apartments at 862 and 866 East South Temple Street, built as two separate residences beginning in 1901 in Federal and Shingle styles.

Cross 900 East Street, past the condominium highrise at 908 East South Temple Street and the Ronald McDonald charity house across the street to your left (north), to the site of the former Rosenbaum house.

20. Rosenbaum House (904 East South Temple Street)

Now a multi-level condominium development, the Rosenbaum house was built for banker Edward Rosenbaum by architects Ware and Treganza, who turned an existing small vernacular house into a quaint Queen Anne cottage. In 1927 Rosenbaum sold his house to Frank Moormeister, a physician. Three years later Moormeister's high-rolling wife was abducted from here and murdered. Organized crime was thought to have been behind the murder, but the assailant was never found. Frank was charged twice in the 1920s for performing illegal abortions.

Continue east along the south side of South Temple Street to the red sandstone pillars marking the entrance to Haxton Place.

21. Haxton Place (940 East South Temple Street)

This exclusive 1909 development was designed to replicate Haxton Place in London, childhood home of Thomas Griffin. His ivy-covered stucco cottage at the end of the cul-de-sac with the organic curve to the bay, and his friend James Keith's house to the west at number 34, appear to be one house but are separated by a 17-inch gap. The space is stuccoed over in the front and back. Original deeds for ownership in this neighborhood precluded people of African or Chinese descent. A number of prominent families chose to live here, including Alta Club president Clifford Pearsall and Governor Simon Bamberger. The restrictions expired in 1930.

Continue east on South Temple Street. At the corner of 1000 East Street you will see, across the street on the southeast corner, the Moreau Medical Building. This is adjacent to Holy Cross Hospital, established in 1882 by Catholic sisters of the Holy Cross. Here miners suffering from lead poisoning were treated.

Turn left and cross South Temple Street to the north. The corner house on your left at 973 East South Temple is one of the first Spanish Revival houses in the city. Notice the rope pilasters, arched windows and doorways, stained glass, and red tile cupola on the stuccoed chimney. The house was built in 1925 by Phillip Wrigley, owner of the Sweet Sixteen retail chain.

Continue north (you are on O Street) to First Avenue. When you reach the corner, notice the white stucco house with grey trim on the northeast corner. This is the Whitney home.

22. Whitney House (903 First Avenue)

At the turn of the twentieth century, books with standard house plans, called pattern books, were popular for people on a budget. Authors of these books mixed styles, as they did in this case blending a French mansardic roof and dormers with Italianate lintels and brackets. The house was built in 1903 by Madison Whitney, founder of Utah Land, Water, and Power Company, and it has since been converted to apartments.

Cross First Avenue and turn right, walking east along the north side of First Avenue toward P Street. The 2-story Allen house on your left, second from the corner of P Street (929 First Avenue), was the residence of liberal Republican Clarence Allen, the state's first U.S. congressman. He purchased this Victorian Eclectic home in 1908. It was built in 1895.

Cross P Street to the Hawley house on your left (northeast corner).

23. Hawley House (953 First Avenue)

The first story of this Shingle Style/Queen Anne was constructed of brick. The upper level displays the typical patterned wood shingling flared over the brick first floor. The house dates from 1890 and was built by Utah National Bank chief teller Cyrus Hawley.

Continue east next door.

24. Silva House (957 First Avenue)

This pattern book design, considered Colonial Shingle Style in 1891, could qualify today as a modern Cape Cod. Note the small, semi-circular window over the porch roof and the huge fanlight over the tall front window.

In 1899 Silva sold the house to Parry Henderson, former territorial chief justice. The next owner was Reuben Farnsworth, son of Philo

Farnsworth, one of the inventors of television. The house now contains apartments.

Continue east a few steps to the Talmage house across the street on your right. You are now on the south side of First Avenue.

25. Talmage House (970 First Avenue)

This 2-story Victorian Eclectic house, with the interesting elliptical window in the tower gable, was built in 1900. Not the most impressive house on the block, it is noteworthy because of its English-born owner, James Talmage. A prominent educator, scientist, and LDS apostle, Talmage was one of Mormonism's most eloquent and persuasive defenders. Among other things, Talmage also accepted the premises of organic evolution, and, in college, experimented with marijuana. Like many of the homes in this neighborhood, the house has been converted to apartments.

Walk east to the southwest corner of Q Street. From here you can see the Freed house diagonally across the street at the northeast corner.

26. Freed House (1007 First Avenue)

This imposing 2-story Shingle Style palace was completed in 1892 and purchased in 1916 by Claude Freed, a golf enthusiast who founded the Salt Lake City Country Club. This house was part of the Darlington Place development—an upscale housing tract. Notice the use of classical motifs and huge gabled roof.

———

☛ Side Trip. Further east, mid-block on your right (south), is the Tracy house (1024 First Avenue). This pattern book house with an inviting upper porch was finished in 1892 and purchased in 1906 by Russel Tracy, a noted philanthropist. Tracy later moved to Second Avenue in Federal Heights.

On the northwest corner, across to your left, is the Coffin house (1037 First Avenue). This elaborate Queen Anne with an onion-dome turret was built in 1896 for Edwin Coffin, a hardware store owner, stock broker, and mining executive. It is the finest example of this style of house in the Avenues.

Return back to the west side of Q Street. End Side Trip.

———

At Q Street and First Avenue, proceed south on Q Street one block to the corner of South Temple Street, passing the beige-brick Victorian home at 27 Q Street (west side), built in 1897 by the owner of the McConaughy Lumber Company.

To your right (west) as you reach the corner is the Town Club.

27. Town Club (1081 East South Temple Street)

The widow of Samuel Walker of Walker Bank built this Georgian-influenced residence in 1909. It was purchased in 1939 by an exclusive women's club. Notice the expansive front porch, paired columns, front-center dormer with a swan's neck pediment, and corbeled chimneys.

At the curb, notice the green electric poles which serviced the trolley cars that once rambled up and down Brigham Street. The first trolleys ran on tracks but were mule-drawn. Electric lines were introduced seventeen years later in 1889, putting 84 mules out of business. Original wooden poles were replaced by steel girders in 1906. The trolley company, founded by Brigham Young, Jr., and two partners in 1872 as Utah Light and Traction Company, evolved into Utah Power and Light, the state's utility company.

Cross Q Street east and proceed east along South Temple Street on the old sandstone sidewalk. Across the street to your right (south) is a string of houses, beginning with the Moran House, that you can see best from this north side of the street.

28. Moran House (1106 East South Temple Street)

English immigrant Patrick Moran purchased this substantial late Victorian style home in 1901, two years after Edwin Mulford completed it. A contractor, Moran then built the Craftsman bungalow to the east at 1108 for his mother-in-law, but she died before the house was completed. Inexplicably the Morans moved into the bungalow and let the larger home stand vacant. Notice the small, semi-circular eyebrow window in the roof of the big house, and, on the bungalow, the fascia boards with flared ends lining the gable. Moran campaigned for city commissioner in the 1920s and—though not solicited—received backing from the Ku Klux Klan. He lost.

Next door to the east, fronted by tall white columns, is the Franklin house.

29. Franklin House (1116 East South Temple Street)

The owner of Yankee Consolidated Mining Company, Norwegian immigrant Peder Franklin built this American Colonial Revival residence in 1899, complete with stables in the rear. Subsequent owners added the fanlight above the door, small balcony, portico, enclosure between the dormers, and stucco over brick. The rear carriage house has also been converted to an apartment.

Continuing east, just past the H-shaped Commodore Apartments on your left, is the Tudor Revival Scheid house.

30. Scheid House (1127 East South Temple Street)

Built in 1907 for Karl Scheid, a professional singer, this substantial house was designed for recital acoustics. When Scheid's wife died, he took a room at the Alta Club. In addition to musical interests, Scheid owned an insurance company.

Continue next door to the Lyne house, now the Brigham Street Inn, on the corner.

31. Lyne House (1135 East South Temple Street)

Walter Lyne, a wool broker, built this 2-story house in 1898. Lyne was orphaned at the age of twelve when his parents, who were seance mediums, mysteriously disappeared. Walter found work as an errand boy at the Brooks Arcade Drug Store, and, later, after he had made his fortune, purchased the drugstore.

The formal architecture mixes Queen Anne massing—rounded bay window and steep dormers—with Neo-Classical details—semi-circular portico, paired columns, entablature, and Palladian window (tripartite, arched in the center). Some of the original woodwork and tile of the interior have been preserved in the bed and breakfast renovation. The house originally included servants' quarters in the basement.

Cross R Street and continue east on South Temple Street. Wasatch Elementary School is on your left, with an underground walkway to the playground across the street to the south. East of the playground is the Lester Freed house (1164 East South Temple Street) with sleeping porch over the entrance facing east. Freed was a bank director who began his career as a bill collector. The house was later converted to apartments, but has since been reconverted to single-family housing.

On your left (north) is the Lynch home.

32. Lynch House (1167 East South Temple Street)

This house was built in 1899 by William Hatfield, a stockbroker, who sold it to John Lynch before occupying it. Lynch directed one of Utah's first ice manufacturing companies. His success is evident in this grand Victorian/Neo-Classical hybrid with a fashionable Palladian window in the upper front gable. The lavish interior included mahogany walls. Later converted to the Queen of Peace convent, the building now houses Sisters of Holy Cross.

East of the Lynch house, at the northwest corner of S Street and South Temple, the yellow mansion with 2-story columns and expansive pediment is the Armstrong mansion.

33. Armstrong Mansion (1177 East South Temple Street)

One of the best examples of its kind on South Temple Street, this temple-fronted Neo-Classical Revival edifice was built in 1911 by banker William Armstrong (not to be confused with his namesake, another banker, the son of Mayor Francis Armstrong). Notice the understated entranceway to the right, facing South Temple Street, compared to the grand, 2-story portico. The architect was Richard Kletting, who designed the state capitol building.

Local folklore tells of a murder that took place here—the husband shooting his wife's young lover who fell out the window and bled to death. Occupants say that at night they hear footsteps racing toward the window.

Cross S Street to the house on the northeast corner.

34. Walker House (1205 East South Temple Street)

This massively-proportioned Shingle Style house with prominent tower and Georgian semi-circular portico was constructed in 1900 for Robert Grant. Joseph Walker, who developed the Walker Mining Company, purchased the house in 1906. The stone retaining wall on the west side is original.

The 1-story Italianate house across the street at 1207 East South Temple Street housed the William Bancroft family. Bancroft was general manager of Union Pacific, Southern Pacific, and Oregon Shortline railroads. He also owned the 2-story Box Style house behind the smaller structure.

At the next corner east (T Street), on your left, is the renovated Terry house.

35. Terry House (1229 East South Temple Street)

This elaborate Georgian Revival house was built in 1908 for Louis Terry with the help of Henry Ives Cobb, the New York City architect who designed the Boston and Newhouse buildings on Exchange Place in downtown Salt Lake City. The house, yard, and brick walls were recently the object of a major restoration. Terry was general manager of Troy Laundry in Salt Lake City. At the corner, notice the bronze sculpture of a bench with hat and umbrella.

Cross T Street and continue east. Across the street to your right, the Box Style Wasatch Zen Center at 1274 East South Temple dates from 1913, and the Knickerbocker apartments next door on the corner at 1280 East South Temple were built in 1911 by the founder of a plumbing supply store. Notice the wooden square columns.

Reservoir Park, east of the Knickerbocker, includes the Salt Lake Arts Council Art Barn Gallery which sponsors art shows, lectures, receptions, and plays. There are also tennis courts, a softball diamond, and a playground.

To your left (1283 East South Temple) is the stately, ivy-covered Mayflower apartments, built in 1927 in the shape of an H, with Spanish roof tiles and railed French doors in place of windows on the second and fifth floors.

At U Street, the white, 2-story, Neo-Classical villa-form house on the northeast corner (1309 East South Temple) was built in 1921 by Lewis Sowles, who became chief underwriter for the Federal Housing Authority.

Turn left and walk north up U Street.

Terry House (IV. 35)

36. Cunningham House (18 U Street)

This Craftsman bungalow on the east side of U Street was designed by LDS church architect Don Carlos Young in 1908. Bungalows became popular about 1905 thanks to Pasadena architects Charles and Henry Greene. The economical, ground-hugging, wide-porched structures were inspired by the colonial houses of India known for their full-length verandas. Bungalows have a front-center dormer, a porch supported by wood or brick columns or battered piers, exposed beams, casement windows, wide eaves, and a front door leading directly to the living room. Arts-and-Crafts details on the Cunningham house include the flared wood fascia and second-story porch railing. William Cunningham had investments in railroad, mining, and insurance.

Continue north to the colonial house with shingled walls on the left at the southwest corner of First Avenue and U Street.

37. Ware House (1184 First Avenue)

Walter Ware was a principal of the architectural firm of Ware and Treganza, who designed the First Presbyterian Church and Ladies' Literary Club. In 1905 Ware treated himself to this gambrel-roofed Dutch Colonial Revival house with rounded and elliptical windows. Ware's father Elijah invented the steam-driven carriage, a precursor to the automobile. Walter's brother William was a Columbia University professor of architecture.

Cross First Avenue and continue north on the west side of U Street. Notice the blue and white Queen Anne cottage across the street at 68 U Street built in 1898 by Jefferson Wilson, a cigar store owner. Next door, at 76 U Street, notice the house with the full-length, second-story balcony framed by square columns. To your left (west), at 75 U Street, is an example of Art Moderne, with its graceful, curved wall and glass bricks at the entryway, flat roof, and white stucco.

To your right (east), on the southeast corner of Second Avenue and U Street, is the Taylor house.

38. Taylor House (98 U Street)

Historian Juanita Brooks once owned this enlarged pioneer vernacular house with its north-south-east-west dormers. Built in 1890 for James Taylor, the house was soon sold to Fort Douglas army officer William Heckman, a Mormon, remembered for his role in the White River Indian massacre. Brooks, who wrote *Mountain Meadows Massacre*, exposed atrocities perpetrated by Mormons and Ute Indians against Missouri immigrants in 1857.

From the corner of Second Avenue, you can see the Jennings house across the street on the northeast corner.

39. Jennings House (1205 Second Avenue)

Reminiscent of an "old Kentucky home" with a wrap-around porch, this American Colonial Revival house was built in 1901 for William Jr.

and Martha Jennings. Notice particularly the pleasing high-contrast color scheme. William Jr. was son of millionaire William Jennings of Devereaux House fame, and Martha was president of the Utah Federation of Women's Clubs.

Cross Second Avenue to the north and turn left (west). The second house from the corner, on your right, is the Steiner house.

40. Steiner House (1175 Second Avenue)

This Shingle Style house was designed in 1902 by Walter Ware's partner Albert Treganza. It was purchased in 1911 by George Steiner, founder of the American Linen Supply Company, director of Walker Bank and Trust, and president of the Chamber of Commerce. This spacious house still sits on about one-half block of land.

Continue west to the house on your right on the northeast corner of T Street and Second Avenue.

41. Warrum House (1153 Second Avenue)

This Box Style house was built in 1905 for Noble Warrum, an editor at the *Salt Lake Tribune* and author of the history *Utah Since Statehood*. He was also a probate judge, state senator, city recorder, Mason, and staunch Democrat. Warrum sold the house in the 1920s to conservationist Harold Fabian who organized the State Park and Recreation Commission, served on the National Park Advisory Board, and helped John Rockefeller preserve Jackson Hole, Wyoming.

Cross T Street and continue west. The second house from the corner, across the street on your left (south), is the Millspaugh house.

42. Millspaugh House (1126 Second Avenue)

This 2-story Victorian pattern book house with the gabled porch and slanted bay was built in 1895 for Jesse Millspaugh, principal of the Salt Lake Collegiate Institute, a Presbyterian college-prep high school which later became Westminster College.

Next door to the west is the plum-colored gingerbread-trim Ferguson house.

43. Ferguson House (1120 Second Avenue)

Built in 1892 by Henry Ferguson, a carpenter, this picturesque, 1.5-story Queen Anne cottage was sold in 1899 to the founder of the Albert Walsh Plumbing Company, which was located behind the home in a separate building. Notice how the lattice work and other detailing create a lively exterior.

Continue west to the corner of Second Avenue and S streets. On your right at 1103 Second Avenue, the quaint stucco house with the octagonal corner bay tower is a pattern book design built for Mary and Isabella Craig.

Turn right at the corner, heading north on S Street. On your right, the 1-story cottage at 124 S Street was constructed about 1896 by Avery

Timms, a builder. Across the street to the west, unnumbered, is a brick carriage house rare to the area.

Continue to the corner of Third Avenue. Turn left and head west across S Street to the second house on your left from the corner.

44. Felt-Lyman House (1084 Third Avenue)

Built in 1895 by Frank Grant, this late Victorian house sold to Charles Felt, then was purchased by Richard Lyman in 1906. The porch was added later. Lyman, an educator and engineer, became an LDS apostle in 1918 but was excommunicated in 1945. His wife, Amy Brown Lyman, served in the state legislature and was president of the Mormon women's Relief Society until her husband's excommunication.

In 1921 the state legislature passed a tobacco prohibition bill. In 1923 the Lymans successfully championed a revision which made tobacco a controlled substance, with revenue accruing to the state. Another Lyman-backed bill six years later banned tobacco advertisements, which was subsequently ruled unconstitutional.

Like the Felt-Lyman house, many of the homes in this area were built by Frank Grant in the 1890s in stylized housing tracts, evident in the similarity of designs.

As you continue west, note the three Grant houses beginning three doors west of the Felt house at 1068 Third Avenue. The house at 1064 was owned by Alfred Peabody, a South African immigrant who was St. Mark's Cathedral organist and Orpheum Theatre Orchestra conductor. The next house west, at 1058, is a Victorian Grant house purchased in 1896 by Edward Mehesy, a furrier and hide tanner. The house was later purchased by Peter Steffens, a cigar maker.

Directly across the street to your right (north) is the blue Clark house.

45. Clark House (1059 Third Avenue)

High school principal Arthur Clark had this tiny Queen Anne built in 1895. Notice the domed tower and fishscale siding on the dormer. A missing corner porch was recently reconstructed. Clark later became assistant district attorney for Utah Territory and then chief justice of the territorial supreme court. Next door at 1053 Third Avenue (unnumbered) was the longtime home of early twentieth-century Mormon polygamist Joseph Musser.

Cross R Street and continue west. The second house from the corner, across the street to your right at 1037 Third Avenue, is another Grant house, built in 1897 as one of the first rental properties in the Avenues. It was later converted to apartments.

The second house from the corner of R Street on your left, at 1018 Third Avenue, is a pattern book design built about 1903 by the owner of a hardware store. Next door, the ivy-covered Victorian tract house was owned by Francis Lyman.

46. Lyman House (1014 Third Avenue)

This house was built by developer John Anderson in 1898 and was the residence of Mormon apostle Francis Lyman, son of renegade LDS apostle Amasa Lyman who joined the Godbeites in 1870, and father of Richard Lyman, whose house was farther up the street.

Unlike most of Anderson's Victorian Eclectic tract houses, this has an Italianate hip roof and bracketed eaves. It also has a rectangular—instead of typically polygonal—bay window.

Next door to the west is the Richards house.

47. Richards House (1010 Third Avenue)

Yet another Anderson Victorian Eclectic tract home, but more typical of his style with the front porch, this one was purchased in 1906 by future Mormon apostle George Richards. Notice the dentiled corner molding.

Next door on the corner lived a former Congregationalist college professor.

48. Tibbals House (1006 Third Avenue)

This Anderson tract home was purchased by William Tibbals when completed in 1898. Tibbals by this time had left the Congregationalist Salt Lake College and amassed a fortune in the Tintic mines in Eureka, Utah, southwest of Utah Lake. Intact is the original iron fence.

At the corner of Q Street and Third Avenue, cross to the northwest corner where the street sign is attached to a telephone pole. Behind a tall chestnut tree is the Hanchett house.

49. Hanchett House (983 Third Avenue)

The Hanchett fortress is one of the largest Box Style houses in the Avenues. This 2.5-story house was built in 1904 for Lafayette Hanchett, president of the National Copper Bank and director of the Federal Reserve Branch Bank. In 1920 he became president of Utah Power and Light.

The house behind and to the north of Hanchett, at 171 Q Street, is a Frank Grant tract structure, built in 1891 by Eva Rogan. Her husband Ernest was an attorney.

Continue north on Q Street to the corner of Fourth Avenue, formerly known as Wall Street for the 8-foot city wall which once reached to the edge of the city cemetery two blocks west on N Street. The 20-mile wall stretched west from here to the Jordan River and south to 900 South Street. The southern portion was never completed.

At this point, you may wish to detour through the cemetery. If not, turn left and walk west, past what used to be the Spiker Tile and Pottery Company building at 976 Fourth Avenue, to the west corner of P Street.

☛ **Side Trip.** Salt Lake City Cemetery was established by order of the Salt Lake Valley high council of the Mormon church in 1849. It is the resting place for gunslingers Jack Slade, Lot Huntington, Hiram BeBee, and Orrin Porter Rockwell. Nine LDS church presidents are buried here. Lester Wire, inventor of the electric traffic light, was laid here. In 1862 the city was rocked by the revelation that sexton Jean Baptiste had disinterred graves for jewelry and clothing, reburying the dead naked. Baptiste's ears were cut off, his forehead branded "Grave Robber," and he was exiled to Fremont Island in the Great Salt Lake. His beheaded skeleton was later found on the island. The cemetery was originally segregated into Mormon, Catholic, Jewish, Japanese, and Chinese sections. There was also a pauper section.

For a tour of some of the nearer grave sites, enter the cemetery on Center Street (across Fourth Avenue to the north) and proceed north to 245 North Street. Turn right. On your left (north), just before the wooden lamppost, is a 6-foot monument, resembling a chess piece, marking where Henry Dinwoodey and his three wives are buried. Dinwoodey founded Dinwoodey Furniture Company in 1869.

Continue east. Before the next lamppost, turn right into the alley that runs through the Jewish plat to the mushroom-capped pillar on the right for Herman Bamberger and the prominent Frederick Auerbach memorial in a wrought iron enclosure further down on the left side. Bamberger was Governor Simon Bamberger's brother. Herman left Germany at age sixteen to avoid induction into Kaiser Wilhelm's army and became a successful Utah merchant. Auerbach founded The People's Store on Main Street in 1864 and was first grandmaster of the local chapter of the International Order of Odd Fellows.

Backtrack to 245 North and turn right, proceeding east. On your left, opposite the utility shed, is the granite memorial carved in the shape of a funeral bier for the George Albert Smith family. Smith was eighth president of the LDS church. A similar monument further east on the same side of the street notes the resting place of Mormon apostle Orson Pratt and five of his wives. Pratt laid out Salt Lake City's streets.

Continue east to Cypress Avenue, turn left and head north. To your right (east), past 250 North Street, beside the juniper bush, is a headstone for Lester Wire, inventor of the electric traffic signal.

From here, continue north to Grand Avenue. Turn left and traverse the length of the plat west to the corner of Center Street. To your right, on the northeast corner of the intersection, fourth row in, are footstones for three wives of Brigham Young's adopted son Royal Barney—Emmeline Rawlings, Mary Pratt, and Agnes McMurrin. A little further north on Center Street are public rest rooms.

On the southwest corner of the intersection of Center Street and Grand Avenue is a pillared tomb under a maple tree where city mayor William Jennings lies. Jennings founded the Eagle Emporium on Main Street and was the city's first millionaire. He and two wives lived in the Devereaux House. The house of one of his widows is now part of the campus of Rowland Hall grammar school.

Proceed south on Center Street to 250 North Street. Turn right and walk west. About 30 steps past the lamppost on your left, shaded by a pine tree, is a small granite stone, capital, and polished ball marking Sarah Daft's grave. Daft's building on Main Street, next to the Kearns building and across from the *Tribune*, housed her real estate company. Her philanthropic work included financing one of the first retirement homes in the city.

Continue west along 250 North Street a few steps. Just north of the walled Moyle obelisk to your right is William Staines's 5-foot marker. Staines, territorial librarian and Brigham Young's landscaper, built what William Jennings later expanded into the Devereaux House.

Continue west along 250 North Street to Central Avenue. If you have seen enough, you can exit the cemetery south (left) on Central Avenue to the church on Fourth Avenue and P Street and continue the tour with number 50 below. Otherwise walk north on Central Avenue, across Grand Avenue, to the rough-hewn James Talmage memorial to your right, on the northeast corner of Central and Grand.

Continue north on Central Avenue to 280 North Street, then turn left. Walk west about five rows of graves past the lamppost to the obelisk on your left surrounded by trees. This is the grave of vigilante Orrin Porter Rockwell.

West of Rockwell's grave is Wilford Woodruff's bier-like monument. Woodruff was the Mormon church president who abolished polygamy. His villa and farmhouse are featured on the Trolley Square and Liberty Park bicycling tour.

Continue west to Main Street. Turn left, proceeding south. After crossing Grand Avenue, you will see John Lollin's large, granite monument mid-plat to your right (west). Lollin was a successful saloon owner.

Continue south to 240 North Street. To your left, on the northeast corner of the intersection, seven rows in, is gunslinger Lot Huntington's footstone in a short row of four under a pine tree.

To exit the cemetery, proceed east along 240 North Street to Central Avenue. Turn right and exit to the south onto Fourth Avenue. A few steps to your left (east) is the corner of P Street and Fourth Avenue where the tour continues. **End Side Trip.**

———

50. Twenty-seventh Ward Chapel (185 P Street)

This 1903 late Gothic Revival church is one of the few historic Mormon chapels left in the Avenues. Notice the octagonal steeple surrounded by minaret-like spires with rough stone trim and corbeled arches over stained glass windows. There is a peacock in relief over the arched entrance. A later 1928 addition to the south is in compatible Tudor Gothic Style. Notice, near the flagpole, the knobbed finials over the arched stained glass windows. Before the chapel was completed, the congregation met in a rented room over a drugstore.

Head south on P Street. The gray wood-frame structure to your left (east) across the street at 170 P Street is a playful 1891 house that was built as a rental investment. The corner tower and round attic windows qualify as Queen Anne adornments.

At Third Avenue, the red brick, bayed side of the house on the southwest corner (149 P Street) is an example of tract Box Style houses built in this neighborhood by Lucy and Adolph Richter—this one in 1903. The house next door to the west at 924 Third Avenue is another Richter tract house.

Turn right and proceed west on Third Avenue. The yellow brick house on your right (third from the corner) is the Nicholle house.

51. Nicholle House (927 Third Avenue)

This Box Style Richter house was completed in 1902 and purchased by Sidney Nicholle, an employee of the Mine and Smelting Supply Company. This was a mixed neighborhood that included working class residents.

Continue west, noticing the light brown brick house with rust trim three houses west at 915 Third Avenue. This is yet another Richter house.

Continue west next door.

52. Houghton House (911 Third Avenue)

The Richters built this modest Dutch Colonial Revival house in 1906, departing from their standard design but including a 1.5-story gambrel roof and side dormers. It was owned by Alice Houghton, a surgeon.

Continue west and cross O Street, noting the cobblestone cottage on the northwest corner to your right (887 O Street). Continue west to N Street. On the northeast corner to your right, the large Box Style, yellow-brick house at 851-855 Third Avenue (unmarked) was built in 1909 as one of the earliest triplexes in the city.

Cross N Street to the third house from the northwest corner on the right.

53. Williams House (825 Third Avenue)

Glen and Charles Miller developed a small tract of land in this area, building four 2-story frame houses. This Victorian Eclectic house has a small, recessed, second-story balcony framed by brick piers. Also notice the dentiled cornice. The house was completed in 1892 and purchased by boot salesman Ernest Williams.

Continue west, past the condominium town houses on your right, to the corner of M Street. Looking diagonally across the street, notice the 2-story flat-roofed duplex (135-37 M Street) on the southwest corner, designed by Richard Kletting in 1909 with his initial on the front wall.

Cross M Street and continue west to the Smith house mid-block on your right.

54. Smith House (765 Third Avenue)

George Smith, an Oregon Shortline Railroad attorney, and wife Euphemia, built this Georgian-influenced bungalow in 1905 on the site of an earlier adobe-and-frame house. It was acquired in 1915 by Jacob and Eva Provol, who ran a branch of the Hudson Bay Fur Company. Notice the swan-neck pediment and lunette window.

Continue to L Street and cross to the west, still on the north side of Third Avenue. To your right, the corner house (735 Third Avenue) is an 1890 brick Box Style structure that was expanded and remodeled in 1902 by Josiah and Harriett Burrows, owners of a Main Street clothing store.

Next door, at 729 Third Avenue, the clean lines of this 2-story brick house with hip roof create a stately appearance for what is actually a 1904 pattern book house. The owner was Frank Castleton of Castleton Brothers General Store.

Continue west to K Street, where you will find a convenience store at the northeast corner. Across the street to your left (southeast), the Wild Rose bicycle shop was built in 1938 as the Gem Grocery and Meat Company. Cross K Street and continue west along Third Avenue. The third house from the corner on your right is the Anderson house.

55. Anderson House (681 Third Avenue)

John Anderson, who built many of the tract homes in the Avenues, constructed this 2-story Victorian abode with rusticated lintels in 1896 and occupied it himself. He sold it three years later to attorney James Darmer who helped found the anti-Mormon American Party which won three mayoral and city council elections. Five years later Darmer sold the home to John Critchlow whose wife, Florence, was a daughter of Mormon church president Lorenzo Snow.

Continue west. Across the street to your left is the Owen house.

56. Owen House (668 Third Avenue)

John Owen, a tailor, sang evenings with the Opera Society, the Mormon Tabernacle Choir, and the Harmony Glee Club. His pattern book Queen Anne cottage was built in 1899, an example of the increasing affordability of small urban homes during the Gay Nineties.

Continue west to the corner of J Street. The green wood-frame structure on your left (southeast corner) across the street, behind the catalpa trees, is the Woolf house.

57. Woolf House (654 Third Avenue)

Samuel Woolf was a Jewish merchant who owned a wholesale cigar business on Main Street. His brother Moss lived next door to the left (east). Notice the frontier western look created by wood window surrounds and accents. The wrap-around porch with lathed balusters, bay windows, and fancy brackets also contribute to this effect.

Cross J Street and continue west. Many of the homes in this neighborhood were owned by merchants. The pattern book Box Style house across the street to your left at 624 Third Avenue was built by grocery store owner David Affleck (notice the four prominent chimneys), and the pattern book cottage next door to the west at 614 was built by wool broker Joseph Kearns in 1906.

Continue west. At I Street, turn left (south) to the first house from the southeast corner. You should be walking south on the east side of I Street.

58. Tuttle-Spry House (128 I Street)

This wood-frame Box Style house with the elliptical window was built in 1901 by Walter Tuttle and purchased by Utah governor William Spry in 1911. During Spry's terms as governor, the state capitol was completed and labor leader Joe Hill sentenced to death. Two Hill supporters attempted to blow up Spry's house the night before the execution in 1915 and again the next year. Spry lost the Republican Party's nomination for a third term in 1916 because of his opposition to Prohibition. Spry had formerly been president of the Farmers and Stockgrowers Bank and U.S. marshall. The house was moved here from its original location at 368 First Avenue. National Register of Historic Places.

Across the street (west) at 133 I Street, the small, blue, wood-frame house with the fancy porch posts was built in 1891 by Christian Orlob, a cabinet maker, who sold it to John Snowball, a teamster.

Continue south. To your left, on the northeast corner of Second Avenue, fronted by stone lions facing Second Avenue, is the Ellis mansion.

59. Ellis Mansion (607 Second Avenue)

This imposing Georgian Revival mansion was designed by Ware and Treganza and completed in 1906 for Adrian Ellis, Jr., a Salt Lake City lawyer specializing in mining law. He sat on the board of directors for First National Bank and Columbia Steel Company. From the 1950s to the 1970s it housed a rest home.

Notice the ornate, bracketed cornice, the crown-shaped chimney flue, and the rosette window in the front gable. Although a structure of this kind may seem isolated, it is only four blocks from the Kearns mansion. National Register of Historic Places.

Turn right onto Second Avenue and head west. The 1940s metal sign signifying the Continental Dry Cleaning Company at 569 Second Avenue belies the 1917 origin of the building and the Continental Cleaning and Dyeing Company that once occupied it.

Across the street to your left at the southeast corner of H Street, with

Ellis Mansion (IV.59)

Ellis Mansion, detail (IV.59)

the chimney facing Second Avenue, is one of the few Prairie homes in the Avenues.

60. Cannon House (86 H Street)

This 1911 hip-roofed Prairie house was built for Radcliffe Cannon, son of Mormon apostle George Q. Cannon, and designed by his brother, Lewis Telle Cannon, and John Fetzer of Cannon and Fetzer architects. Notice the brown brick, leaded art glass in geometric patterns, and horizontal window bands.

Cross H Street and continue west along Second Avenue. Across the street on the left (south), at 520 Second Avenue, the white brick house with gray lintels was built in 1904 and shutters added later. The 1898 house next door to the west, at 516 Second Avenue, has Stick Style decoration, including an exposed wood roof over the porch. A pioneer brick cottage once stood next door at 514 Second Avenue but was replaced by this Victorian brick structure with stained glass transoms, shingled gable, and columned porch.

Cross G Street west to the chapel.

61. Twentieth Ward Meetinghouse (107 G Street)

This Neo-Classical-influenced, L-shaped Mormon chapel was built in 1924 and restored in the 1980s. Notice the emphasis in the quoined corner trim, the narrow, vertical windows, dentiled cornice, and Palladian entrance. National Register of Historic Places.

Directly across from the chapel to the south is a small but striking Italianate house with brown trim.

62. Wallace House (474 Second Avenue)

That the original owner, Howe Wallace, was a carpenter is evidenced by the artisanship in this house, such as the fancy woodwork over the corner window, including pendants. Also notice the mansard roof, the wood frieze, and the heavy lintels over the widows. The house was built in 1888.

Continue west to the first house after the chapel.

63. Staines House (461 Second Avenue)

One of the few Victorian homes in the city with Romanesque details, this was the 1892 dream house of William Staines (not to be confused with William Staines of Devereaux mansion fame). It was designed by Walter Ware. Notice especially the round arches, brick texturing, dentiled belts, and large chimneys. There are also gables and shingled siding typical of Victorian eclecticism. The house was converted to apartments in the 1920s.

Continue west to the corner of F Street and cross west, passing the youth hostel to your right. The Bateman house is to your left (south across the street).

64. Bateman House (424 Second Avenue)

This 2.5-story Shingle Style home, with bell-shaped dome and Palladian window, was built in 1891 for William Bateman, one of Utah's first telegraphers and manager of the Saltair Railroad Company. The house has since been converted to apartments.

Continue west to E Street. Turn left and proceed south. The greatly-altered 2.5-story Queen Anne across the street to your right (west) at 87 E Street was considered one of the finest homes in the Avenues when it was built in 1890 for Oregon Shortline attorney Parley Williams.

To the left, at 82 E Street, is a bricked-over adobe residence dating from the 1800s which was renovated in 1909 as a hardware shop.

Across the street, at 77 E Street, the gray and white Tudor bungalow was designed by architect Louis Telle Cannon for his mother Martha in 1910. Martha was one of the many wives of Mormon leader George Cannon.

Next door to the south, the huge, old Craftsman, now a fourplex concealed by trees at 75 E Street, was built around the turn of the century by Louisiana-born district court judge Thomas Marioneaux.

At the corner of First Avenue, turn right (west) and cross the street to the church.

65. Tabor Danish Evangelical Lutheran Church (387 First Avenue)

This late Gothic Revival chapel was designed by Theodore Lauridsen in 1909 for a Lutheran congregation. Notice the New England influence in the tall, thin, coned bell tower topped by a cross. The church was purchased by a Baptist congregation in 1911 and renamed Central Baptist Church. It was later converted to office space. Note the parsonage to the rear.

Continue west along First Avenue. The 3-story Hawthorne House apartments next to the church on your right (north), at 379 First Avenue, date from 1908. Continue west.

At the southeast corner of D Street and First Avenue, you will recognize the broadside of the Daynes house which we saw earlier on the tour (number 4 on the map). Turn right at D Street, heading north.

66. Cahoon House (66 D Street)

Among other things, contractor John Cahoon was president of the Salt Lake Saddlery Company and loved horse racing. Behind this substantial Victorian home (stained glass windows still intact) was a 2-story barn for Cahoon's prized horses.

Two doors north is the home of one of the most prominent nineteenth-century western photographers.

67. Savage House (80 D Street)

The original adobe section of this late Italianate house was built in 1871 for nationally-recognized photographer Charles Savage and his two wives. Notice the vintage lilacs in the front yard. The hip roof and bracketed cornice, as well as the rectangular massing, are typical Italianate features. Notice the art glass transom over the front door. The front porch and narrow shutters are later renovations.

Later the house was occupied by Savage's son-in-law, J. Reuben Clark, Jr., U.S. undersecretary of state, ambassador to Mexico, and councillor in the Mormon church presidency. Clark sympathized with Germany during World War II and was an outspoken opponent of the atomic bomb.

Continue north to the corner, turn left, and cross D Street to the west. The store on the southwest corner was built in the 1930s as the People's Market. Continue west to the corner of C Street. The beige stucco house with brown trim to your left at the southeast corner of C Street and Second Avenue is the Sansome house.

68. Sansome House (86 C Street)

This house began as a Federal design but underwent several face lifts in the way of wood lintels over the windows and other eclectic elements. Charles Sansome, who built the house, managed a Mormon cooperative store.

From the corner where you stand, you can view the duplex across the street (southwest corner) at 87 and 89 C Street, with green brick, white columns, and two oval second-floor windows. The duplex was built in 1905 by mine equipment specialist Mike McGee. From your vantage you can also view a yellow brick house with a white columned portico two houses south of the duplex. This 2-story Box Style house was the residence of Mormon intellectual Brigham Roberts.

69. Roberts House (77 C Street)

As a ranking LDS leader, Roberts argued for acceptance of Darwinism and other progressive ideas, for which he was silenced. In other ways, Roberts reflected his time and culture. He spent four months in prison in 1889 for polygamy and, in 1898 when elected to the U.S. House of Representatives, was denied his seat because he had two wives. In the state legislature he opposed women's suffrage. Notice the house's Dutch-stepped front gable, reminiscent of Brigham Young's Nauvoo, Illinois, home.

If you would like to take a shortcut at this point, continue west one block along Second Avenue to pick up the tour at number 81 below. Otherwise continue with number 70.

Cross C Street west to the duplex, then cross Second Avenue to the north to the Young house on the northwest corner. It is a Box Style house with colonial touches. It faces Second Avenue.

70. Young House (299 Second Avenue)

This house was built by Willard Young in 1907. He was a son of Brigham Young and president of LDS University. Mormon apostle Anthony Ivins later acquired the house. As president of the Juarez,

Mexico, congregation, Ivins harbored Mormon polygamist fugitives in exile for more than a decade at the turn of the century. He was subsequently appointed an LDS apostle and later a counselor to Mormon church president Heber Grant.

Proceed north. Next door (north) to the Young house on the west side of C Street is a grand 2-story Victorian house.

71. Foster House (111 C Street)

This Victorian Eclectic home dates from 1900. The owner, William Foster, was a popular folk singer as well as a skilled carpenter. Notice the diamond-shaped window above the portico and the fishscale dormer. In 1924 Foster's wife died in the house when her clothes caught fire in front of the open stove.

Next door to the north is the Neslen house.

72. Neslen House (117 C Street)

This is one of the few vernacular dwellings remaining in the Avenues, based on a Greek temple form with a T-shaped addition. Its tasteful elegance reflects its original owner, Samuel Neslen, who built it in the 1870s.

Continue north to Third Avenue, crossing north to the short, yellow-brick Victorian house on the northwest corner.

73. Dinwoodey House (153 C Street)

Designed by Richard Kletting for William Dinwoodey in 1895, the distinctive round tower is upstaged only by the later grasshopper weather vane. Dinwoodey formed the mining stock brokerage of Lawrence and Dinwoodey. As a young man he worked for his father Henry's furniture company. National Register of Historic Places.

Continue north. To your left (west) toward the end of the block is a string of polygamous houses.

74. Robinson Houses (177, 179, 181, 185 C Street)

A devout Mormon polygamist owned this row of 1-story vernacular cottages begun in 1873. Fortunately for William Robinson, his occupation as a carpenter allowed him to keep up with his expanding household. Notice that cottages 179 and 181 are connected.

At the corner of Fourth Avenue, turn left (west). Notice the red brick house with blue trim to your right (north).

75. Brown House (271 Fourth Avenue)

This Victorian Eclectic house was a wedding gift from William Brown to his daughter Helena in 1891. Her husband, William Romney, founded Romney & Ryan Printing Co. which featured the first linotype machine in the area. The most unusual feature of the house is the four-sided bell tower placed centrally rather than to one side.

Continue west to the corner of B Street and Fourth Avenue, past Carlton Towers (266 Fourth Avenue), and turn left (south) down B Street. Across the street on the southwest corner of B Street you can see the fishscale gable of brick mason Joseph Chapman's residence poking above the trees (187 B Street). Next door to the south, in red brick and rust, green, and yellow trim, behind the original stone wall, is the Beer House.

76. Beer House (181 B Street)

Notice the brightly colored bowling-pin balustrades of William Beer's 1899 Victorian Eclectic home. Beer was a respected physician who attended to German prisoners of war at Fort Douglas during World War I. Notice the etched leaded-glass transoms. The house was designed by Richard Kletting.

To your left (east), the red brick house with the umbrella tower and ornate porch is the Evans house.

77. Evans House (174 B Street)

Richard Kletting also designed this Queen Anne house in 1889 for John Evans, general manager of the Mormon-owned *Deseret News*. His son, Richard, a Mormon apostle, is remembered for Sunday sermons delivered as part of the weekly Mormon Tabernacle Choir broadcast.

South of the Evans house is the Richard Kletting neighborhood mini-park. The best-known of early Utah architects, German-born Kletting also served on the city's planning and zoning commission and is credited with promoting park landscaping throughout the city. He was killed by a car in 1943.

Across the street, the duplex at 167 and 169 B Street was the home of Robert Patrick, owner of Patrick Dry Goods. Patrick was a Mormon bishop for twenty-eight years.

Two houses further south, standing near the northwest corner of Third Avenue (157 B Street), is one of the oldest houses in the Avenues. This Gothic Revival relic with the spear-tipped finial was built in the 1860s by Mormon polygamist William Bell Barton, a clerk in the LDS church's Presiding Bishop's office. The north addition is recent.

To your left, at the northeast corner of Third Avenue, is the 1888 home of Ichel Watters, with white stucco and green trim.

78. Watters House (253 Third Avenue)

Watters was a Jewish jewelry merchant who was beaten with brass knuckles during the boycott on non-Mormon commerce. He refused to leave the territory and not only survived but thrived both in retail and as a leader in the rabbi-less B'Nai Israel congregation, where he provided encouragement and support to other Jewish immigrants. Notice the distinctive window treatment and austere, clean lines of the wall that would now be considered Art Moderne. The house is altered Italianate.

Cross Third Avenue to the south. The 2-story structure on the southeast corner is the Ellerbeck mansion.

79. Ellerbeck Mansion (140 B Street)

Built in 1892 for a polygamous wife, this spacious house represents the transition from Victorianism to more restrained Neo-Classicism. Notice the fan window over the north entrance, the widow's walk, and ornate brackets. Also note the entrances facing both Third Avenue and B Street.

Thomas Ellerbeck, Brigham Young's chief clerk, died three years after building this home for his wife Henrietta, who eventually sold the house to William Armstrong, son of Salt Lake City mayor and bank president Francis Armstrong. Francis was also president of the trolley company after anti-polygamist legislation placed it in receivership. William became a state senator and president of Salt Lake Livery and Transfer Company and of his father's Utah Commercial and Savings Bank.

Continue south along B Street. Mid-block, across the street to your right (west), is a yellow stucco cottage.

80. Ferguson House (121 B Street)

This Victorian Eclectic cottage was built in 1887 for Dr. Ellen Brooke Ferguson, a house physician at the old Deseret Hospital and a leading suffragette. Later she organized the Woman's Democratic Club in Salt Lake City and was the only female delegate at the 1896 Democratic National Convention.

Continue south. The John Edwards house on your left at 116 B Street began as a 1-story brick cottage in 1891; a second story was added in 1896, and the porch was added in 1924 when the house was converted to a duplex.

Continue south. At Second Avenue, cross the street diagonally to the southwest corner to the Priscilla Paul Jennings house. This is one of four buildings housing Rowland Hall-St. Mark's School. Rowland Hall was a boarding school, St. Mark's a day school. The two merged in 1964.

81. Jennings House (87 B Street)

Jennings had this magnificent Neo-Classical Revival Style house built about 1901 after her millionaire husband and mayor William passed away and the Devereaux House seemed too large. Priscilla, a polygamous wife, was a prominent leader in the Mormon women's Relief Society. The Episcopal church purchased the house in 1956. Note the two gabled bays, the pediments with modillions, the heavy cornice and dentil molding, and the enclosed porch.

Walk south on the west side of B Street past the playground to the wrought-iron gate mid-block. Enter the gate on your right to the foot-path through campus. Proceed west. The Caine house is immediately on your left (south).

82. Caine House (67 B Street)

Joseph Caine, an insurance executive, had this house built in 1888. This grand, early-Victorian domicile, notable for its polychromatic brick and stone decoration, was purchased by the Episcopal church the same year as the Jennings house.

Follow the footpath further west through the quadrangle to the open-stage patio. On your right is the Watt homestead.

83. Watt House (205 Second Avenue)

On approaching the Watt house, you will see the east-wing replica of the original structure and the rear-addition cafeteria and classroom building. The east and west wings were joined in 1910 by a 2-story hall with an upstairs chapel. The original adobe home of George Watt, secretary to Brigham Young, was built in 1862. Watt later defected to the Godbeites.

Facing south from the Watt House, you will notice—beyond the outside theater—a passageway through DeWitt Van Evera Hall to the street. Walk through this corridor and down the steps to First Avenue. Turn left and walk east to the Rawlins house on the northwest corner of First Avenue and B Street.

84. Rawlins House (233 First Avenue)

Joseph Rawlins was a "Jack (lapsed) Mormon" son of a Mormon bishop who had a successful law practice and was elected a U.S. congressman in 1892. He is credited with having negotiated statehood for Utah. Rawlins's Victorian Italianate home is best known for its 2-story, slanted bay windows with bowed eave. Notice also the oxbow lintels. The retaining wall outside the home is original and helps to enclose the campus in a 1-block compound. National Register of Historic Places.

At the corner of First Avenue and B Street, turn right and cross First Avenue south. You are at the rear of the cathedral where the tour began at South Temple Street and 300 East. This concludes the Avenues and South Temple Street tour.

V.
University of Utah and Fort Douglas

DISTANCE: 6 MILES   TIME: 5 HOURS

Begin at the visitor parking lot south of the University Bookstore. To reach the parking lot by car, head east from the city on 400 South Street, which curves after 900 East to become 500 South Street. Continue in the left turn lane past Rice Stadium to 1580 East Street. Turn left at the traffic signal, heading north. Turn left onto South Campus Drive (400 South Street) heading west, moving immediately into the right turn lane and turning right at the library/bookstore sign at 1500 East. Drive north to the middle of the lot. The rate is $5 per day.

By bus, take number 4 north at designated signs on the east side of South State Street between South Temple Street and 400 South Street. The bus destination reads Fort Douglas or Hogle Zoo. Buses run about every 20 minutes. The fare is 65 cents. Disembark at the Campus Hub stop on South Campus Drive. Cross South Campus Drive to the north, turn left, and walk half a block to the library/bookstore parking entrance at 1500 East Street. Turn right and walk to the middle of the parking lot.

Position yourself on the sidewalk that runs east and west through the parking lot, lined with lampposts. From where you are standing, you can see a number of prominent historic buildings. Looking south, you can see the yellow brick, gabled side of the old Basketball Hall and the press box and lights of Rice Stadium behind it.

1. Basketball Hall (South Campus Drive)

This World War II-vintage sports arena, now the Einar Nielsen Field House, is where the first campus basketball games were held. It also provided space for student assemblies, such as the 1968 lecture by Timothy O'Leary and Sidney Cohen debating the merits of LSD. It no longer serves these purposes but does include tennis courts, an indoor track, racquetball courts, and weight rooms.

2. Robert L. Rice Stadium (South Campus Drive)

Across South Campus Drive, connected to the field house by a tunnel, is the football stadium. It began in 1901 as Cummings Field with bleachers for 6,000 fans. In 1927 a concrete and earth stadium was erected to accommodate 20,000 spectators. Later the stadium surface was lowered, the bleachers expanded to a horseshoe shape, and dressing rooms added. Robert Rice donated astroturf, a press box, and lighting. The stadium now holds 35,000 fans.

UNIVERSITY OF UTAH
AND FORT DOUGLAS

FEDERAL
HEIGHTS

MERRILL
ENGINEERING
BUILDING

1580 EAST

UNION BUILDING 56

MARRIOTT 4 LIBRARY

SOCIAL AND BEHAVIORAL SCIENCES CENTER 3

58

57

SOUTH CAMPUS DRIVE

1500 EAST

500 SOUTH

X FINISH
X START

55

5 P

P

6

13

7

1 UTAH RICE STADIUM 2

PRESIDENTS' CIRCLE

14

12

15

11

10

8 PIONEER MEMORIAL THEATRE

HALL

17

UNIVERSITY STREET

EAST

200 SOUTH

300 SOUTH

400 SOUTH

9

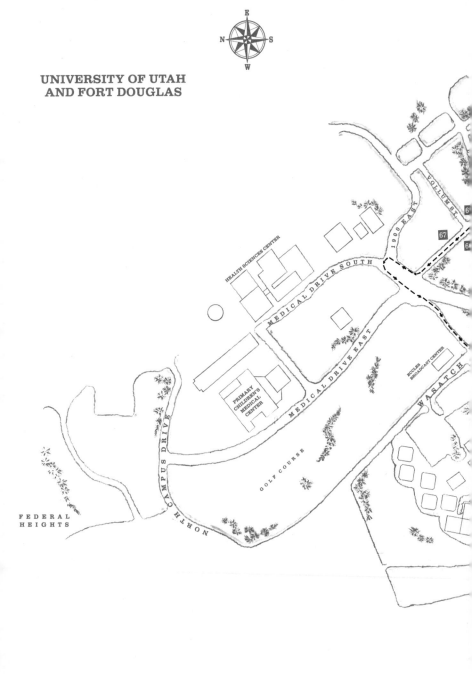

UNIVERSITY OF UTAH
AND FORT DOUGLAS

FEDERAL
HEIGHTS

FORT DOUGLAS

FT. DOUGLAS BLVD.

HEMPSTEAD RD.

POTTER ST.

CHASE ST.

OBERLAND ST.

STILWELL FIELD

62

63

61

60

63

59

SOUTH CAMPUS DRIVE

HUNTSMAN CENTER

500 SOUTH

V. A. MEDICAL CENTER

To the southeast is the tallest building on campus—the Social and Behavioral Science tower—and the Marriott Library.

3. Social and Behavioral Science Tower (University Campus)

Reflecting the New Brutalism trend in architecture, designers left the building materials exposed—in this case mostly concrete. The 13-story building was completed in 1971. As you tour the campus, this building can serve as an orienting landmark.

4. J. Willard Marriott Library (University Campus)

Notice how the library appears to be a free-standing block in the style of New Formalism. The original $6-million structure was completed in 1968 with floating-terrace reading areas, a central atrium with skylights, an auditorium, and a reception room furnished with imports from Barcelona. A mid-1990s $34-million expansion nearly doubled the total gross square footage to almost 500,000. The new 2-story addition was built entirely underground.

To the north you can see the orange brick side of the University Bookstore, completed in 1961. In the mid-1960s the store was targeted by a student group calling themselves B.I.T.C.H.—Bookstore Improvement Through Committee Harassment—which felt the facility was inadequate. In 1976 the store was expanded to double the size. You can see the roof of the student union building in the distance over the top of the bookstore.

Immediately west of the bookstore, almost concealed by trees, is the vine-covered rear entrance to the old campus dining hall.

5. Dining Hall (University Campus)

The Dining Hall was erected in 1920 in a modest Second Renaissance Style. Now called the Performing Arts Building, it includes dance studios, classrooms, and a theater in the round.

West of the Performing Arts Building is where until 1994 the U's original 1906 gymnasium stood. By 2000 the site should feature a new biology building.

6. Old Gymnasium Parking Lot (University Campus)

The school's first gymnasium, in Second Renaissance Style, was completed in 1906. In the latter half of the century it served the ballet and modern dance programs, but the primitive dressing rooms and rickety showers proved an allurement for voyeurs until it was renovated in 1985.

South of the old gymnasium parking lot is Building 44, which houses faculty offices. South of that—west of where you stand—is a new dance facility.

7. Alice Sheets Marriott Center for Dance (University Campus)

This impressive structure appeared in 1987 as the third campus building in the country devoted exclusively to dance. It was designed by FFKR Architects, who also designed Abravanel Hall where the Utah Symphony Orchestra performs. The Marriott Center for Dance includes a 400-seat auditorium.

Proceed west on the walkway between the Marriott Center for Dance and Building 44. Pass through the openings in the concrete wall of the oval garden. The Biology Building is on your right (north) and the Henry Eyring Chemistry Building annex to your left (south). As you emerge from the oval garden, the brick and concrete Life Science Building will be on your right (north) and a white biology quonset hut to the left (south).

Notice the botanical label on the box elder tree to your right opposite the biology hut entrance. The campus is an arboretum, and many of the trees carry such labels. Botany professor Walter Cottam and "disciples" began an ambitious and unauthorized landscaping project after World War II when the campus exploded with new students and classes were held in makeshift government barracks. Cottam's efforts were later recognized by the university, and the state legislature eventually designated the entire campus as the Utah State Arboretum. The grounds boast over 7,000 trees of 350 varieties.

Continue west, passing the horse chestnut tree on your left to the railed sidewalk, passing the 1920s William Stewart Training Building on the right (now housing the anthropology department). Descend the staircase to the left, turn right, and follow the path past the Pioneer Memorial Theatre's side doors to the front doors facing west.

8. Pioneer Memorial Theatre (University Campus)

Like Pioneer Memorial Museum across town, Pioneer Memorial Theatre is a loose replica of the historic Salt Lake Theatre which was demolished in 1929. This modern variation, completed in 1963—thirteen years after the museum—was partially funded by the Mormon church and designed by church architect Harold Burton. The theater is home to Pioneer Theatre Company (PTC), the only fully professional drama company between Denver and the west coast. There is a full-time resident staff of thirty-two, with over 300 theater artists employed annually.

Follow the walkway in front of the theater west to University Street (1320 East). To your left (south) is the Law Building and, beyond that on the northeast corner, Carlson Hall—the old women's dormitory (now housing the history department). Cross University Street and continue west on 300 South Street one block to 1300 East Street.

Turn right at 1300 East Street and proceed north. Along this block are favorite student and faculty hangouts such as Market Street Broiler in the old fire station across the street to the west.

9. Fire Station Number 8 (258 South 1300 East Street)

This fire station, built in 1930, was renovated in 1983. It is one of the city's three oldest fire stations still intact. Notice the interesting round-headed windows and light, airy interior. National Register of Historic Places.

Continue north to the corner of 200 South Street, noticing Waking Owl Bookstore across the street to your left at 208 South in a house built in 1908. The enclosed front porch is a later addition.

At the corner of 200 South Street, turn right (east) to return to campus. You will pass University House on the right (1310 East), an apartment complex built in 1927. Next door is The Pie Pizzeria, downstairs at 1320 North.

Continue north, crossing University Street and entering campus through the sandstone gates erected in 1913. Originally the gates held two bronze doors, since replaced by wrought iron. Follow the path east. This is Presidents' Circle (220 South) and features the oldest buildings on campus. The buildings have since been renamed for past university presidents, but their original historical designations are retained for this tour.

Turn right at the sidewalk intersection leading south and cross Presidents' Circle (220 South) to the old Thomas Library, now a museum.

10. George Thomas Library (Presidents' Circle)

This 1935 library, built under George Thomas's administration, houses the Utah Museum of Natural History, featuring biology, geology, paleontology, and anthropology exhibits, as well as "touch" exhibits. Open Monday-Saturday, 9:30 a.m.-5:30 p.m.; Sunday and holidays, 12:00 m.-5:00 p.m. Adults $2, children $1.50, seniors $1.50. Notice the triple-arched entry and the cornice lined with lions' heads.

Turn left, and continue east along Presidents' Circle. The next building you encounter on your right—with the arched entry—is the Normal Building, one of the oldest structures on campus, renamed the Alfred C. Emery Building in 1980.

11. Normal Building (Presidents' Circle)

The Normal College (college of education) found a home in this Second Renaissance Revival edifice in 1901, designed by Richard Kletting, architect for the state capitol. It now houses the family studies programs. The tall chimneys serve as air vents. Notice the sandstone keystones and other carved details, and the modern concrete and glass addition to the east. Alfred Emery served only two years as president in the turbulent early 1970s.

The next building on the circle is the school's first museum, later renamed in honor of university president James E. Talmage, who served three years beginning in 1894.

12. Museum (Presidents' Circle)

In addition to two natural science museums, this 1902 building with the prominent portico housed the biology department—Talmage's discipline before he was elevated to university president—and various laboratories. For anatomy students, the county physician provided unclaimed bodies to be used as cadavers. The third floor assembly room doubled as the school's gymnasium, with adjacent baths. Notice that the museum is similar in design and layout to the Normal Building. Museum architect Samuel Dallas followed Kletting's design, adding double Corinthian sandstone columns, a fan-shaped transom, and a small balustraded porch at the entrance.

At the head of the circle, with a massive, stately portico, is the Neo-Classical administrative building, now the John R. Park Memorial Building. Notice that the Thomas Library borrowed the lion's-head cornice from this building.

13. Administration Building (Presidents' Circle)

This monument was built in 1914 to house administrative offices and was later named after the first president of the university, John Park, who held an M.D. from New York University. There is a statue of Park in the alcove to the left of the entrance. A grand granite staircase leads to the entrance. The lobby includes marble walls and staircase, and behind the building a recently-added arbored patio provides a protected walkway to the Student Services Building to the east. The Park Building was designed by Lewis Cannon and John Fetzer.

When Park was hired in 1869, the school, which was called University of Deseret, had been closed for seventeen years for lack of funds and had not yet offered university-level classes. On paper the school was chartered in 1850 and still claims to be the oldest university west of the Mississippi, as does Willamette University in Oregon. But under Park's leadership the school became a legitimate institution of higher learning, though he retired before the school changed its name to University of Utah or moved to its present campus.

Continue around the circle heading west. The Applied Research Building, set back from the circle, was built in 1901 as the Mechanical Building, where classes were taught in carpentry, metal forging, and steam engineering. The next building housed the first campus library, again in Second Renaissance Style, known now as the LeRoy E. Cowles building.

14. Library (Presidents' Circle)

The first library, known as the "L," was completed in 1900, but with only 13,000 volumes the library filled less than half of the first floor. The rest of the building was occupied by liberal arts classrooms and offices. The communications department is now located here. LeRoy Cowles

Administration Building (V.13)

served as university president for four years, beginning in 1941. Notice the off-center entrance identified by a porticoed arched doorway.

Next door to the west is the old Physical Science Building which once housed chemistry and physics. It is now the John A. Widtsoe building, named after the Norwegian immigrant who served as president for five years from 1916 to 1921.

15. Physical Science Building (Presidents' Circle)

Two years after its dedication in 1899, this building was nearly destroyed by fire—only the foundation and walls were left standing. It was restored in 1902. Today it serves the mathematics department. Notice that the old library and the Physical Science Building are matching twins with the old museum and Normal Building across the way. This building was designed by Richard Kletting.

Standing at the far corner of the Physical Science Building, you can see the next two buildings on the circle, the Neo-Classical Revival Kingsbury Hall and the old Student Union, now Gardner Hall. If you decide to take a closer look, return to this spot before continuing the tour.

16. Kingsbury Hall (Presidents' Circle)

This spacious concert hall was built in 1930 with some Egyptian Revival elements in the porch articulation. Its exterior skin is composed of warmed, colored terra-cotta. Interior murals were painted by Depression-era WPA artists. Although many concerts are now held in the newer, larger Huntsman sports arena, many people feel that the finest concerts on campus are still held here. The large rear addition was completed in 1996.

It is ironic that such a prestigious hall should be named after the university's least popular president, Joseph T. Kingsbury, whose career ended in 1915 when he fired four professors for making deprecating remarks about his administration. Seventeen other professors resigned in protest, an investigation was conducted by the Association of University Professors, and Kingsbury was forced to resign.

17. Student Union (Presidents' Circle)

The Student Union building was completed a year after Kingsbury Hall, though work came to a standstill for a few months when funds ran out. When a larger building was completed in 1957, this building was converted to a performing arts center. It now houses music department offices, classrooms, practice rooms, and a small recital chamber. It was named after President David P. Gardner in 1980. The architects for Kingsbury and Gardner halls were chosen by competition. Like Kingsbury, Gardner Hall is a formal, symmetrical structure with classical styling and terra-cotta exterior.

From the corner of the Physical Science (Widtsoe) Building, follow the sidewalk north between the Physical Science Building and Kingsbury Hall. Continue north, passing the Physics Building on your right (east) and walk under the James C. Fletcher Building skywalk which connects the building's west wing lecture hall with east wing laboratories.

When you emerge at 100 South Street, turn right and walk east. Notice the stuccoed vernacular Tri-Delta sorority house across the street to your left (1431 East), second from the corner of Butler Avenue. This side of campus is known as fraternity row, and town/gown friction erupts here occasionally. Besides toga parties and pranks, this neighborhood has been the site of two molotov cocktail bombings, four house fires, and in 1970 the base camp for two Sigma Chi's who were shot by a cemetery guard during a late-night hazing stunt. Neighbors have lobbied to legislate the Greek houses out of the area, but an uneasy truce restricts fraternities and sororities to a 4-block area.

Continuing east, notice the Tudor Style Chi Omega sorority house next door to the Tri-Delts.

18. Chi Omega House (1435 East 100 South Street)

Chi Omega received its national charter in 1913, making it the oldest sorority in Salt Lake City. The house was built in 1927 with accommodations for six coeds—only a fraction of the sorority membership—and a ground-floor ballroom. In 1944 the Chi O's made history by posing for *Life* magazine with what school administrators thought was "undue exposure of their feminine underpinnings." Originally the sorority limited membership to 50 percent Mormon.

An Elizabethan Style house, next door to Chi Omega on the southwest corner of South Wolcott and 100 South streets, houses the Pi Beta Phi sorority.

19. Pi Beta Phi House (1443 East 100 South Street)

This is actually two brick houses, connected in 1962 by a glassed-in "breezeway" and additional bedrooms costing $95,000. The house accommodates twenty-two coeds. The sorority was nationally chartered in 1928.

At the corner of 100 South and South Wolcott streets (1455 East), cross 100 South Street to the north and proceed up Wolcott on the east side of the street. The Sigma Nu brotherhood owns the house to your right on the northeast corner.

20. Sigma Nu House (95 South Wolcott Street)

This International Style house was built about 1935 for the Sigma Nu's with concrete donated by an alumnus. Fraternity houses are generally financed and managed by alumni house corporations with help from national organizations. Sigmu Nu was chartered in 1924.

North of Sigma Nu is Phi Delta Theta.

21. Phi Delta Theta House (85 South Wolcott Street)

This brick fraternity house was erected in 1962 at a cost of $95,000.

It houses thirty-four men who were originally supervised by a house mother. The Phi Deltas received their national charter in 1915.

Across the street to your left is the Finkelstein house.

22. Finkelstein House (74 South Wolcott Street)

Herman Finkelstein built this classical bungalow in 1915. The columns are not original. Finkelstein was general manager of Western Furniture Company, the first store in the valley to sell hand-operated household washing machines.

Since about 1970 the house has been occupied by various fraternities—Sigma Phi Epsilon since 1987. Early on the Sig Eps earned a reputation as rowdies with their annual Roman party and "purple shaft" award to the sorority of their choosing.

On the southwest corner directly north of the Finkelstein house, in the stately brick Elizabethan Revival structure, is the equally infamous Beta fraternity.

23. Beta Theta Pi House (70 South Wolcott Street)

The Betas received their national charter in 1912. They moved here from Butler Avenue in the mid-1980s, when the house was vacated by the sorority that built it in 1927. In the 1960s the Betas boasted the best pajama parties on campus, and such extravaganzas as an annual Robin Hood theme party continue. Notice the steep-pitched roof, half-timbering, and multi-colored brick typical of Elizabethan Revival.

Cross north at the intersection with Federal Way (40 South), noticing the Kappa Sigma fraternity house on the northwest corner.

24. Kappa Sigma House (1435 Federal Way)

The Kappa Sigs purchased this house in the mid-1930s to the dismay of neighbors, especially after hazing activities and an annual French Sewer Party. But when the house went on the market, no one else bid on it.

In 1988 a handful of Kappa Sigs was arrested when, according to police, "The frat guys were having a real good time at their little party and they were out in the street and I guess they were dropping their drawers and the neighbors were starting to complain." When fifteen police officers arrived to quiet the revelers, they were mooned as well.

Continue north. On your right, at 33 South Wolcott Street, is the Burton house.

25. Burton House (33 South Wolcott Street)

Walter Burton founded Burton Coal and Lumber and was vice president of Three Kings Consolidated Mining Company. He was a member of the Hoo-Hoos carpenters club and, having worked for a brother's architectural firm, designed and built his own home about 1923. He and four partners developed portions of the neighborhood through their National Real Estate and Investment Company. The house fell to the Greeks in 1934, when it was purchased by the Kappa Kappa Gamma sorority, Delta Eta chapter.

Continuing north, the house across the street to your left is the Findling house in Second Renaissance Revival style.

26. Findling House (26 South Wolcott Street)

Jack Findling was president of the Boston Store on South Main Street. The most fashionable Salt Lake City shops at the time were named after coastal sites. Findling's competition included the New York Store, California Store, and Vermont store. He established himself here about 1923, and about 1940 sold the house to Merle Heitzman, manager of the Silver King Mine in Park City. It continues to be a private residence.

At the corner—where there is an island in the middle of a turn-around—keep to the right on the east sidewalk as it curves slightly around the head of South Temple Street and continues north. You will notice that street numbers which were decreasing are now increasing, marking the end of South Wolcott and beginning of North Wolcott Street. You have entered Federal Heights, one of the city's most exclusive neighborhoods. Ironically, this elite subdivision was once called Butcherville due to nearby slaughteryards. Much of the land was later purchased by Jewish merchant Charles Popper, and the neighborhood became Popperton Place. It was further developed by James Hogle, who called it Federal Heights due to its proximity to Fort Douglas.

On your right, at 8 North Wolcott Street, notice the pink Mediterranean style house with red tile roof and horse post near the sidewalk, built in 1925 by Herbert Sanford, founder of Western Dental Supply. His wife Hazel ran the business after his death and lived in the house until 1975.

To your left, the Elizabethan Revival house at 1441 East South Temple Street is the McDonald residence.

27. McDonald House (1441 East South Temple Street)

"McDonald feeds the world chocolates" was J. G. McDonald Chocolate Company's slogan when it employed 400 people and exported powdered chocolate and cocoa. Their hand-dipped chocolates were considered the state's best. Out of his father's mercantile business, James began manufacturing chocolate in 1862, and his factory on 300 South Street, which now stands vacant, passed through three generations of McDonalds. The house remained in the McDonald family until 1987.

Continuing north, follow the bend in the road to the 2-story red brick home behind a brick wall to your right. This is the famous Fisher house.

28. Fisher House (36 North Wolcott Street)

Frank Fisher, of Fisher Brewery, was one of the first to build in Federal Heights. This red brick Georgian Revival house with the prominent portico was erected in 1911. During Prohibition alcohol was stored in the basement behind a false wall. After Prohibition, Fisher brand beer was the most popular in town. It was eventually purchased by Lucky Lager. As you continue north, notice the portico over the driveway leading to the garage further back. Utah legislator Genevieve Atwood, whose mother was a Fisher, was raised in this house. Frank Fisher was the son of brewery founder Albert Fisher.

Continue north a few yards, then cross North Wolcott Street west to the 2-story bungalow on the southwest corner of the North Wolcott-Sigsbee Avenue intersection.

29. Donoher House (51 North Wolcott Street)

William Donoher, chief of staff at Holy Cross Hospital, built here in 1922. In 1938 ownership passed to Pi Kappa Alpha, chartered in 1912. The fraternity was temporarily suspended by its national sponsor in 1964 for "trumped up charges of drinking and gambling," then nearly lost their lodge in 1971 to fire. Rather than restore this shingled house, they moved to University Street and the house reverted to a private residence.

At the corner, turn left, crossing Sigsbee Avenue to the west. Walk about two steps north to the intersection with Perry Avenue and turn left, proceeding west on the south side of Perry Avenue to the fork in the road. The Sullivan house is on the right.

30. Sullivan House (1425 Perry Avenue)

Arthur Sullivan, a devout Catholic and deputy commissioner of Franklin Roosevelt's Farm Credit Administration, built this Mediterranean Revival house in 1927. He later sold it to university president Calvin Giddings. Notice how the combination of gables, bracketed eaves, chimneys, keystones, and stuccoed walls create a distinctive charm. The windows are Gothic.

The Spitko house is to your left—the stuccoed bungalow with a shake roof.

31. Spitko House (1422 Perry Avenue)

August Spitko, president of Carpenter Paper Company, immigrated from Austria in 1880. Although bungalows were popular because of their affordability, this 1923 custom, eclectic bungalow combines an attractive stone foundation, ample porches, and a multi-level roof that sets it apart from tract houses.

Cross Perry Avenue to the north mid-block, following the sandstone wall west to the corner of Laurel Street (unmarked). From here you can see the polygonal bay with yellow casement windows and shake roof, and the misshapen brick walls, of the Smith house across Laurel Street to your left, partly concealed by maples.

32. Smith House (55 Laurel Street)

George and Euphemia Smith established themselves in this modified Prairie home in 1916 when they moved here from Third Avenue. The clinker brick—overcooked and discarded as scrap—was picked up from the brickyard without cost. During the Arts and Crafts movement, the varied color and misshapen quality of over-kilned brick was popular, and the brick proved to be stronger than run-of-the-mill. The organic look was a reaction to the formal extravagance of Victorian architecture. The entrance is to the south side of the house under a portico.

Turn right and walk north on Laurel Street, past the Federal pioneer house behind the tall hedge, to the Prairie-School Bradley house to your right on the southeast corner of Laurel and Second Avenue.

33. Bradley House (96 Laurel Street)

About 1897 Cora Bradley built a small brick house on this lot. Twenty years later the house was purchased by Francis Pyke, owner of a lace and sewing needle store. Pyke added a northern addition, a porch, and an extended entry. The house was later occupied by Davis Bitton, a prominent Utah historian.

At the corner of Second Avenue and Laurel Street, cross Second Avenue north. Turn right, proceeding east a few yards. To your left (on the north side), set back from the street, is the red-tiled Schubach carriage house.

34. Schubach Carriage House (1305 Second Avenue)

Richard Schubach, a jeweler, remodeled this carriage house about 1949 to give it a Mediterranean look. He seems to have bought the carriage house from Russel Tracy, who owned the red-tiled brick mansion next door on the corner of Alta Street and Second Avenue.

Walk a few steps east to the Tracy mansion on the northwest corner of Alta Street.

35. Tracy Mansion (1315 Second Avenue)

This multi-colored, iron-oxide brick structure is an expansion of a 2-story Victorian house built here in 1895, combining Prairie architecture with red-tile roofing. The extensive remodeling overseen by Utah architect Walter Ware in 1915 concealed all traces of the original structure. Russel Lord Tracy, founder of Tracy Loan and Trust, financed the remodeling. He moved here from a more modest house on First Avenue. Notice the variegated brick patterns, broad overhanging eaves, and stained glass windows.

Continue east a few steps to the corner of Alta Street. Turn left and walk north to the corner of Third Avenue, passing the gabled side of a brick English town house (1326 Third Avenue) on your left, built in 1920.

Cross Third Avenue and continue north one block toward Fourth Avenue. To your right, at 174 Alta Street, is Utah tax commissioner Roscoe Hammond's 1932 residence.

At Fourth Avenue, where the sidewalk ends, turn right and cross Alta Street to the east, then continue a few yards north to the intersection at Arlington Drive (250 North). Turn right and walk east along this shady, sycamore-lined lane, noticing the Tudoresque house across the street to your left with the red tile roof.

36. Holden House (1353 Arlington Drive)

John Holden, state auditor, built this English Tudor cottage in 1925. Notice, besides the characteristic half-timbering, stuccoing, and irregular façade, the sloping roof—simulating a drooping thatched roof—and the tall chimney with clay chimney pots.

Continue east. To your right, the modest American Colonial Revival frame house with three dormers facing the street is the Freed house.

37. Freed House (1366 Arlington Drive)

In 1886 Simon Bamberger, who would later become governor, established a bathhouse resort called Lakeside on the shores of the Great Salt Lake north of the city. When the lake receded, the resort was moved to a grassy meadow surrounding two artesian ponds four miles east. The park closed during World War II, but in 1946 Robert Freed and Ranch Kimball purchased the park and opened Lagoon Amusement Park which has experienced steady growth since then. Freed built this house a few years before acquiring the park. Like other Utah establishments, Lagoon excluded blacks until the late 1940s.

Next door to the east, the unnumbered cottage with the stuccoed front and saltbox roof on the east is the Burnham house.

38. Burnham House (1376 Arlington Drive)

This organic dwelling—falling somewhere between French Norman and Tudor design—belonged to John Burnham, commandant of Utah's naval reserve battalion, after moving here from South Wolcott Street. Notice the slate roof, clay chimney pots, double-window dormer, and narrow window east of the entrance.

The yellow-stucco cottage directly across the street to your left at 1373 Arlington Drive (number not visible from the street) was built in 1925 by banker John Moser.

Directly east of Moser's house on the north side of Arlington Drive is the Roberts house, a white brick house with decorative green shutters.

39. Roberts House (1383 Arlington Drive)

Jules Roberts, vice president of Mountain Fuel, built this Colonial Revival house about 1937. Notice the delicate fanlight in the arched entrance.

Continue east, following the curve in the road. Two doors east of Roberts's estate, on the north side of the street, is the brick Vrang house with yellow clapboard siding and tall central chimney. (Do not be confused by the numbering on the south side of the street, which by this point does not correspond to the numbers on the north side.)

40. Vrang House (1397 Arlington Drive)

In the mid-1920s geologist Chris Vrang decided on an architectural style resembling an English cottage. Notice the gambrel roof, brick base, and large dormer. The house was later purchased by attorney Beverly Clendenin, president of the University Club. Vrang's son, described as a good boy who "never smoked or drank," shocked the neighborhood in 1952 when he boarded a crowded airliner and killed a stewardess who had spurned him, then shot and killed himself.

The Westcott house is two houses east of the Vrang house.

41. Westcott House (1425 Arlington Drive)

This is an example of the upper-scale tract houses built in the 1920s by developer James "Jimmy" Hogle. The first owner was Warren West-cott. Notice the unbroken pitch of the roof over the bay, creating the impression of a lean-to addition to a Federal base. Also, notice the recessed window. Overall an eclectic design, the prominent detailing seems Colonial. Other houses in the neighborhood have a similar design, such as the one to the west of the Clendenin house.

Hogle, whose father owned a Main Street saloon, was a Yale- and Columbia-educated mining engineer who worked with Enos Hall, Daniel Jackling, Thomas Kearns, and David Keith. He opened investment brokerage offices in Salt Lake City, Beverly Hills, San Diego, and elsewhere, and developed 100 acres in the Federal Heights area. Jimmy's wife Mary was a health-food promoter and animal rights activist. In 1926 the Hogles donated their farm at the entrance to Emigration Canyon to the city for its zoological gardens. Hogle is memorable not only for his business acumen but his inability to master the reins of an automobile. Until his license was revoked, he was known to be the most dangerous man on the road.

Two houses further up the street to the left (north) is the Kelly house.

42. Kelly House (1445 Arlington Drive)

This 1925 English Cottage Style house was one of Jimmy Hogle's investments that he sold to attorney Wallace Kelly, later assistant attorney general of Utah. Kelly sold the house in the 1940s to banker and Alta Club president Melvin Dye. The home is now owned by former University of Utah provost James Clayton.

Continue east a few yards to Fairfax Road. Turn right and walk a few more yards south to Penrose Drive. At Penrose Drive, turn right (west) and walk a very few steps to Circle Way (1450 East). Cross Penrose diagonally to the modest Ranch Style house on the southwest corner. This is the Moyle house.

43. Moyle House (1436 Penrose Drive)

Contractor Vigo Madsen is responsible for this 1948 house, though it may have been an investment only. It sold four years later to insurance executive James H. Moyle. Moyle was also president of United Oil Company and director of Utah Parks and Recreation. His son, Henry D. Moyle, became an LDS apostle. His brother, James D. Moyle, was U.S. assistant secretary of the treasury.

In the 1960s this was the residence of Mormon church president Harold B. Lee, remembered for creating the Church Security Plan—later known as the Welfare Program—during the 1930s Great Depression, and the LDS Correlation Committee which oversaw the bureaucratization of Mormonism. Notice the cupola on the garage to the south.

Turn left and proceed south along Circle Way. To your left, just before the road begins to curve west, is the Monterey Style Rosenblatt house.

44. Rosenblatt House (1444 Circle Way)

Joseph Rosenblatt chaired the local Federal Reserve Bank and was president of a manufacturing company. He built this stuccoed Spanish Colonial home in 1932. About twelve years later he moved two blocks south to Military Way. University English professor William Mulder, editor of *Among the Mormons,* later owned the house.

Next door to the south is the Burton house.

45. Burton House (1442 Circle Way)

Working as a bank teller, Edward Burton discovered that his eyesight was failing. Suddenly unemployable, he founded a company that became the most successful securities brokerage in town, underwriting 95 percent of the valley's municipal bonds and financing Utah's sugar beet industry. He built this rich brown-brick Tudor Revival with the fairy castle dormer in 1927. Notice the elaborate door and window surrounds, the reverse dormer over the entrance, and the clay chimney pots.

In 1965 the house transferred to Weyher Construction Company founder Robert Weyher. In the late 1970s Weyher rescued Westminster College from collapse. He was also a benefactor to Zion National Park Historical Association.

The decorative Federal Revival manor next door (south) is the Burrows house.

46. Burrows House (1440 Circle Way)

Alma Burrows built next door to his father-in-law, Edward Burton, the same year as Burton. Burrows succeeded his father-in-law as president of Burton and Company and later became a director of Beneficial Life. Notice the broken-scroll pediment over the entryway and three prominent Palladian windows recessed in brick archways with granite keystones.

The Elizabethan Revival house next door (south) was built by Fred Moreton in 1927.

47. Moreton House (1438 Circle Way)

Moreton owned a securities and insurance company bearing his name. Notice the decorative door-surround, double chimneys with clay pots, half-timbering, and the sweeping roof line of the projecting gable section.

Back to Colonial architecture, proceed next door (south) to the Wright house.

48. Wright House (1434 Circle Way)

Clarence Wright built here in 1930. He founded Wright and Sons department store, the largest in the city, which was later purchased by J. C. Penney. Wright married the daughter of the Dinwoodey Furniture Company owner. When they moved to Santa Monica in the 1940s, they sold to the son of Arthur Frank, clothing chain founder. Notice the wrought iron balcony extending to the rear of the house.

Continue southwest. As you near Hildon Avenue, the palatial Cates mansion rises on the southwest corner.

49. Cates Mansion (1430 Circle Way)

The most impressive Second Renaissance mansion in Utah, this stuccoed, 16-room, 6-bath showpiece was built in 1928 by Louis Cates, vice president of the Utah division of Kennecott Copper. It was sold two years later to David Moffatt, Cates's successor at Kennecott when Cates became president of Phelps Dodge Corporation.

Notice the red terra-cotta roof, copper rain gutter and drain pipes, gargoyles at the corners under bracketed eaves, rococo door trim, arched windows, and eastern balcony over the garage. The interior includes walnut floors, marble bathrooms, gold leafing, and a search-for-the-holy-grail mural extending over three walls.

Turn left onto Hildon Avenue, where there is no sidewalk but few cars. The house directly in front of you as you reach the T-intersection at Military Way is the Mueller mansion, now the official residence of the president of the University of Utah. The northern addition, with a round, white chimney and glass wall, is most visible. Cross the street to the south side of Military Way.

50. Mueller Mansion (1480 Military Way)

George Mueller immigrated to Utah from Germany in 1890 and opened a bakery on South State Street where he produced European-style bread and pastries in a wood-burning stove. He opened the Royal Cafe on Main Street in 1905. Eventually he was wholesaling 50,000 loaves of bread a day to restaurants and groceries from two plants, including the first machine-wrapped bread in town which he marketed as "Table Queen Bread," wrapped in a "prom-pretty, four-color, wax-paper gown."

Mueller built this sprawling, Neo-Shingle Style house in 1930. Later he would donate 1,000 acres of land in Bountiful, Utah, for Mueller Park, and extensive property in Mill Creek Canyon to the Forest Service. Joseph Rosenblatt moved here from Circle Way about 1944, later donating the house to the university for use as the president's residence.

Turn right and proceed west on Military Way. West of the president's residence is the red brick Hewlett house.

51. Hewlett House (1470 Military Way)

Mormon Tabernacle Choir director Lester Hewlett built this Federal Revival manor two years after Mueller established himself next door. The current owner is former Wall Street financier Ian Cumming, now of Leucadia Financial Corporation, located in the Keith mansion on South Temple Street. Notice the matching eastern addition to the house.

Continue west on Military Way. The cobblestone English cottage three homes west of the Hewlett estate is the Harris house.

52. Harris House (1422 Military Way)

This was one of the earliest homes on the street and one of the few rock houses in the area. It was built in 1926 by Fisher Harris, city attorney, director of the Metro Water District, and author of *One Hundred Years of Water*. During the drought of 1934 Harris promised he would never again allow the golf courses to go dry. True to his promise, he oversaw massive reservoir and aqueduct expansion.

Continue next door (west) to the Clarke mansion with the long brick staircase leading from the street.

53. Clarke Mansion (1418 Military Way)

This grand, wood-frame American Colonial Revival mansion has seen a host of prominent people come and go, including Robert Clarke, Utah Copper Company executive; Fred Auerbach, railroad director; and James White, part owner of Manhattan's General Motors Building. In 1975 the house was acquired by attorney Brooke Grant.

According to news reports, Grant once held interest in Talcott Company, which neighbor Ian Cumming helped him unload in a securities exchange buy-out. Cumming reportedly acquired controlling interest to the company. Grant subsequently sued his neighbor for $4.5 million and won. Grant's interest in Talcott was allegedly acquired through an individual later linked to the Vatican Bank scandal.

Continue west, hugging the sidewalk to the left where it bulges at the Second Avenue turnaround. Stopping for a moment, look back over your right shoulder to see the Walker mansion at the head of the Second Avenue island.

54. Walker Mansion (1401 Military Way)

Senter Walker held extensive ranching interests in Utah and Idaho, owned the Walker Iron Mining Company, and developed land. In 1926 he built this mansion for himself and family in Mediterranean Revival Style.

Continue west, bearing to the left on Sigsbee Avenue. Just a few yards past the intersection is a path that will take you back to the university. Before the path is a chain link fence and clump of maples on your left. On the far side of the path is a tall, black, wrought-iron fence. Turn left, enter the unmarked alley with the neighborhood mini-park to the left, following it south to Federal Way (40 South).

Toward the end of the alley, there is a parking lot to your left, followed by stone pillars marking the entrance to campus. Turn left onto Federal Way and walk one-half block east to North Campus Drive (1500 East), passing the Kennecott Research Center on your right where atomic research is conducted in partnership with the university.

Cross North Campus Drive to the east and follow the sidewalk that winds a bit to your left, leading to the steel and glass Merrill Engineering Building. Turn right and cross the foot bridge. Follow the sidewalk south, keeping to your right. You will be traversing campus from north to south, passing the Engineering and Mines Classroom Building on the left (east), followed by the Energy and Minerals Research complex with a satellite dish and buffalo-relief façade, also to the left. On your right (west) is the 8-story, $8-million William Browning tower, housing the College of Mines and Earth Sciences.

Depending on the season, you should be able to see the Tanner Fountain ahead of you between the Student Services Building on the right (west) and the University Union on the left (east). Continue south to the fountain plaza.

55. Student Services Building (University Campus)

This is an easy building to spot with its multi-dimensional concrete, limestone, and glass façade with external staircases, wood awnings, and roof-top sun screens. It reflects contemporary International Style, designed by architect Neil Astle in 1983. The $4-million building includes rooftop plazas with trees and tables. The building houses admissions, records, and loan offices.

56. A. Ray Olpin University Union Building (University Campus)

The University Union is a 1957 Prairie brick-and-glass building designed in 1949 but not completed until 1955 due to funding problems. The building was expanded in 1964 and remodeled in 1972. It includes student government offices, ballrooms, a food court, and rest rooms.

Continue south past the student union building, veering slightly to the left onto the diagonal path that runs further south, past the granite boulders on your left and an emergency telephone on your right. To your far right is the bookstore. In the distance to the southwest, as you continue, is the Social and Behavioral Science tower rising high above the Marriott Library.

When you reach the library, zig-zag a bit to the left to continue south along the east side of the library, through Marriott Plaza. In season there will be water cascading over a cement wall to your left. East of the fountain is Orson Spencer lecture hall, built in 1955 as the humanities building. It was named after the Baptist minister-turned-Mormon who was university chancellor for three semesters of the failed University of Deseret.

As you leave the plaza, you will see the red brick David Eccles School of Business ahead, a bit to your left (east), funded by a $15-million endowment from descendants of the founder of First Security Bank. Before the building's 1991 dedication, the school was known among faculty as "Operation Bootstrap School of Business."

The cement and glass Art and Architecture Center is directly west of the Eccles building. Just before you reach these buildings, at the round flower bed in the middle of the walk and another emergency telephone box, turn right (west) and descend the stairs toward the Social and Behavioral Science highrise. Below the stairs is a decorative black-steel, free-standing canopy. Walk underneath and turn left to the entrance to the Minimalist Style Utah Museum of Fine Arts.

57. Utah Museum of Fine Arts (University Campus)

The museum houses an impressive—and expanding—permanent collection of world art, including Navajo textiles, southeast Asian sculptures, Japanese screens and prints, Chinese ceramics, and objects from African, Oceanic, and pre-Columbian cultures. Touring exhibits are also featured. Open Monday-Friday, 10:00 a.m.-5:00 p.m.; weekends, 2:00-5:00 p.m.; closed holidays.

At this point you may wish to take a shortcut and drive (or ride the bus) to Fort Douglas, which is on the east side of campus. Otherwise skip ahead to continue by foot.

———

☛ Shortcut. If you are continuing to Fort Douglas by car, descend the stairs leading to the Social and Behavioral Science tower. At the bottom of the second flight, turn right and angle down four steps, walking north past the delivery dock to the Marriott Library on your right. Then turn left into the parking lot where you began the tour.

Exit the parking lot and turn left (east). Proceed east on South Campus Drive, following it around a slight curve all the way to Wasatch Drive. Cross Wasatch Drive to the east through the traffic light to enter Fort Douglas. Cross Chase Street and continue east 1/2 block on Hempstead Road to the parking lot to your left. Return by foot to the corner of Chase and Hempstead and continue the tour at number 59.

If you are continuing to Fort Douglas by bus, descend the stairs to the Social and Behavioral Science tower and turn left, heading south between the museum and the Social and Behavioral Science Auditorium annex. At the parking lot, turn right and proceed south to South Campus Drive. Cross the street to the Campus Hub stop. The bus goes directly into Fort Douglas to the corner of Chase and Hempstead, where the tour continues at number 59. **End Shortcut.**

━━━━━

To reach Fort Douglas by foot, circle back a few steps to the northeast corner of the museum. Head south along the east wall of the museum to the skywalk connecting the two wings of the Art and Architecture Center, walking under the skywalk and through the courtyard between the two wings.

58. Art and Architecture Center (University Campus)

This $4-million center was completed in 1971. The east wing holds the College of Architecture and the west wing the College of Fine Arts, connected by a small library. Forty north-light studios were incorporated into the design, and a separate building to the south houses ceramics and sculpture workshops. The exposed concrete exterior, with some brickwork, is an example of New Brutalism, designed by Edwards and Daniels Architects.

As you emerge from the courtyard, climb the stairs to your left (opposite the sculpture studio annex) and follow the sidewalk east. In the distance to your right is a geyser fountain, and ahead on your left is the round Francis Armstrong Madsen business classroom building. You are now traversing campus from west to east.

On your right is a parking lot. Beyond this, looming above the roofs of the Public Safety Building and the Veterans Administration Medical Center, is Mount Olympus. South of Mount Olympus are the usually snow-capped peaks overlooking the ski resorts of Big and Little Cottonwood canyons. On this side of Mount Olympus are the peaks overlooking Parley's Canyon on the way to historic Park City. The gap in the hills ahead of you (east), a bit to the right, is Emigration Canyon, where the Donner Party, and later Mormon immigrants, forged their trail into the valley.

As you continue east, you will pass the Garff and Bennion education classroom buildings on your left (north). At the far end of the parking lot, follow the sidewalk as it veers to the right (southeast). To your left is the west wing of the Health, Physical Education and Recreation complex (HYPER). As you follow the sidewalk southeast you will approach the Jon M. Huntsman Center, used for university basketball and gymnastics events and music concerts.

Ascend the flight of stairs in front of you leading to the Huntsman Center. At the top of the stairs, turn left and begin circling the center to the east. To your left, between the east and west wings of the HYPER complex, you can see the Natatorium indoor swimming facility. Natatorium means "place of swimmers" in Latin.

From here you also should be able to see the Health Sciences Center on the hill to the east. The University Hospital is most prominent at the far left (north), followed by three brick classroom buildings and the Wintrobe Medical Research Building behind them. To their right, the red brick building with the turquoise windows is the Eccles Institute of Human Genetics, fronted by the College of Nursing. To the right, the long cement structure is the Biomedical Polymers Research Facility. To the extreme right, barely peaking above the trees, are the twin Medical Plaza Towers which provide housing for medical students.

Continue circling the Huntsman Center to the second flight of stairs on the east side. Turn left, climb the stairs, cross the street that leads to the parking lot, and walk east along the row of war-surplus barracks to your right. During the post-World War II enrollment boom, the university acquired about seventy military barracks as temporary housing. Some of these have been retained for Air Force ROTC, extension programs, and overflow personnel.

As you reach the end of the barracks, you can glimpse the senior officers' quarters across the street to the east at Fort Douglas (now Stephen A. Douglas Armed Forces Reserve Center). Follow the sidewalk to your right to the intersection of Wasatch Drive and South Campus Drive.

Cross Wasatch Drive east, enter the fort, and continue east, keeping to the left (north) side of the street to the corner of Chase Street and Hempstead Road. You will pass a red-brick double barracks to your right (Building 100) dating from 1939. East of the barracks, across Chase Street, is an old fort stable (building 101)

59. Fort Stable (Hempstead Road)

This 1886 stable accommodated 96 horses and mules. It has been converted into a warehouse, but the hayloft remains intact. The central section of the stable is constructed of rich red local sandstone typical of many of the fort's buildings. The two frame wings provided space for stalls and storage. Not open to the public.

Turn left, proceeding north along Chase Street. To your right is an old parade ground; to your left, an 1884 sandstone brake shop (building 28). You can tell how old base buildings are by construction materials used. The original fort consisted of log cabins, adobe houses, and wood frame buildings. Beginning in the 1870s these were replaced by more permanent red sandstone, followed by red brick in the twentieth century.

At Potter Street, turn right (across Chase), heading east. To your left is Stilwell Field. The two sandstone buildings ahead to your right date from 1875. The second one you encounter, with the full-length veranda, is the fort museum (building 32).

60. Fort Douglas Museum (Potter Street)

Fort Douglas—originally Camp Douglas, named in honor of Illinois senator Stephen A. Douglas—is a 120-acre Civil War garrison founded in 1862 by the Third California Volunteer Infantry ordered here to defend mail routes and telegraph lines and assure that Utah remain in the Union. At first troops were quartered in tents and dugouts, but these were quickly replaced by log and adobe structures.

Later the fort held "prisoners of war"—300 German nationals found living in the United States at the outbreak of World War I, along with socialists, pacifists, and an assortment of "radicals." During World War II, Germans, Italians, and Japanese were confined here, some of whom are interred in the fort cemetery. After Pearl Harbor the U.S. Army's Ninth Service Command transferred here from the San Francisco Presidio for greater security. Much of this history is captured in museum presentations. Open Tuesday-Saturday, 10:00 a.m.-4:00 p.m. (closed for lunch).

Continue east a few steps to the Fort Douglas Historical Park on your right just past the museum, with a statue of the fort's founding officer.

61. Patrick Connor Statue (Fort Douglas Historical Park)

Patrick Edward Connor was born in Kerry, Ireland, immigrated, and enlisted in the U.S. army at age nineteen. He was wounded in the war with Mexico and discharged to join the California Gold Rush, later becoming postmaster of Stockton, California. When the Civil War erupted, he re-enlisted. Arriving in Utah, Colonel Connor's first report to his commanding officer in San Francisco foreshadowed hostility: "It would be impossible for me to describe what I saw and heard in Salt Lake. So as to make you realize the enormity of Mormonism, suffice it that I found them a community of traitors, murderers, fanatics, and whores. The people publicly rejoice at the reverse to our arms and thank God that the American government is gone, as they term it, while their prophet and bishops preach treason from the pulpit. Federal officers are entirely powerless and talk in whispers for fear of being overheard by Brigham's spies. Brigham Young rules with despotic sway and death by assassination is the penalty of disobedience to his command."

Connor wanted to arrest Young but could not receive permission from San Francisco. Undeterred, he trained his cannons on Young's house downtown and temporarily stationed guards a block away from Young's house. Connor began the first daily newspaper in the territory, the *Union Vedette*, which propagandized the northern view of the war and encouraged non-Mormons to immigrate to Utah to exploit mineral wealth, which Connor felt would "revolutionize the odious system of church domination which has so long bound down a deluded and ignorant community." Connor's troops were assigned prospecting missions, and they found rich silver veins in Little Cottonwood Canyon to the east and Bingham Canyon to the west.

Meanwhile Brigham Young ordered the mayor to declare the camp a nuisance because of its proximity to the city water supply, but this scheme failed. Demonstrating the contempt Connor felt for Young, Connor had his soldiers break into the city jail to release a comrade who had been arrested for assault. Meanwhile Young established a ring of informers to monitor activity at the fort and report church members suspected of conducting business with Connor. Women seen near the camp were excommunicated. Ironically Connor and Young never met.

That Connor and his troops were trigger-happy is indicated by the murder of four Shoshone caught stealing horses in 1862, their first year in the territory. Shoshone returned the favor, murdering a group of miners. Connor retaliated by leading his troops on a midnight march to Bear River, attacking an Indian encampment there and leaving 300 men, women, and children dead and seventy tepees destroyed. This action resulted in Connor's promotion to brigadier general.

Continue east to Ft. Douglas Boulevard, crossing east to the sidewalk. From here you can see the ten sandstone duplexes lining Officers Circle further east and north.

62. Officer Duplexes (Officers Circle)

The Gothic Revival gables, tall dormers, and wood, spear-headed finials on these 1876 T-shaped quarters are striking. Each duplex has three chimneys and original verandas. The ground floors consisted of a long entrance hall with a living room and parlor to one side and a dining room and kitchen to the other, with bedrooms upstairs.

Turn left, heading north on Ft. Douglas Boulevard, to the bandstand gazebo on your right and cannon on your left.

63. Gazebo and Cannon (Stilwell Field)

The octagonal gazebo was used for open-air martial band concerts. Behind the flagpole to your left, notice the cannon aimed at the city—Brigham Young's house—as it would have been during the Civil War. The cannons were fired when Connor was promoted to brigadier general and created a panic in town. Unaware of the custom, Mormon minute-men mustered at Young's residence.

Continue north. At the intersection of de Trobriand Street/Officers Circle and Ft. Douglas Boulevard, on the left, is another barracks, dating from 1876. Cross Officers Circle, continuing north. To your left you can see the east side of the old post headquarters, which faces north (building 49).

64. Post Headquarters (Ft. Douglas Boulevard)

The headquarters was built in 1876, originally in a U-shape. The building now serves the Fort Douglas Military Club.

Cross Lewis Street to the north. Across the street to the left, on the northwest corner, you can see the old stairway which used to lead to a trolley stop, now bearing a "Chapel Glen" sign. Before the trolley was brought this far east, the gully was a branch of Red Butte Creek. To your right, on the northeast corner of Lewis Street, is the old Bachelor Officers Quarters (building 5).

65. Bachelor Officers Quarters (Ft. Douglas Boulevard)

Bachelor officers enjoyed this comfortable, L-shaped, red brick building with seven chimneys. Notice the double balcony with fancy balustrades. Also, notice how well the red brick harmonizes with the sandstone structures found throughout the fort. The quarters have since been converted to offices.

Continuing north across Vollum Street, to your left is the old clapboard chapel (building S-48).

66. Post Chapel (Ft. Douglas Boulevard)

This chapel was built in 1884 to replace a temporary cabin-tent that was the valley's first non-Mormon house of worship. Notice the square bell tower typical of Gothic Revival, topped by a "witch's hat" steeple roof and Celtic cross. Also notice the pair of lancet windows on the tower wall, repeated on the chapel walls. The church is still in use today. The horizontal siding is not original.

Continue north. On your right, set back from the street at the northeast corner of Vollum Street, was General Connor's quarters.

67. Connor House (Ft. Douglas Boulevard)

Built in 1876 for the commanding officer, Connor spent part of his tenure here. More elaborately detailed than the other fort quarters, this house was originally a simpler, 1-story, L-shaped, Gothic Revival structure. Over the years various additions have produced a more spacious and ornate home. It has since housed the fort surgeon and offices.

☛ Shortcut. If you arrived by car or bus, this ends your tour of the University of Utah and Fort Douglas. To return to your car, retrace your steps south along Ft. Douglas Boulevard to Potter Street. Turn right (west) and go past the museum and adjacent building to the parking lot on your left. To return downtown, exit the parking lot onto Hempstead, turn right (west), continue west across Wasatch Boulevard, and follow South Campus Drive west.

To return downtown by bus, backtrack south along Ft. Douglas Boulevard, crossing Potter Street, to the unmarked street that angles over to Hempstead Road with the Fort Douglas Historical Park to your right. Turn right on Hempstead and proceed west to Chase Street. The bus stop back to the city is opposite the spot where you descended upon arrival at the fort. **End Shortcut.**

————

To exit Fort Douglas by foot, continue walking north, passing three other houses, to the gate. Walk around the gate. Turn right, walking a few yards to cross 1900 East Street to the east. In front of you is the College of Pharmacy. Turn left to cross Medical Drive South to the north at the crosswalk, then backtrack west to Medical Drive East.

Cross west and follow the asphalt path that winds west, skirting the university golf course, past the Dolores Eccles Broadcast House (KUER-FM, KUED-TV) on the right, to Wasatch Drive.

Cross Wasatch Drive to the west (straight ahead), then cross the small lane (Ballif Road) to the dormitory sidewalk directly in front of you. Proceed along the sidewalk to the south side of the dorms, continuing west. Angle to the left after the brick utility shed with the overhanging green roof. Continue west a few more steps, then turn left to cross Ballif Road to the round bed of flowers.

Turn right and walk west along this landscaped promenade to the Social and Behavioral Science tower. On your left are a softball field and the east and north wings of the HYPER complex. On your right, after two more oval flower beds and a soccer field, is the new Language and Communication building. Continue west.

After another bed of flowers you will arrive at the Social and Behavioral Science tower. Descend two flights of stairs, turn right, and angle down four steps, walking north toward the bookstore and approaching the parking lot where you began. This ends the University of Utah and Fort Douglas tour.

BICYCLING TOURS

VI.
Trolley Square and Liberty Park

DISTANCE: 5.5 MILES   TIME: 1.5 HOURS

1. Trolley Square (602 East 500 South Street)

Trolley Square and its Mission Style car barns today boasts a variety of specialty shops, restaurants, and movie theaters. Notice the distinctive curvilinear parapets. Trolley Square was originally the site of the territorial fairgrounds, but beginning in 1907, 144 trolley cars daily rolled out of these barns on steel tracks, powered by overhead electrical cables. In 1933 the trolleys were replaced by electric buses which ran until 1944. In 1966 local developers began a $10-million renovation, which was completed in 1971. The large metal frame arch at the north end was the original marquee for the Capitol Theatre downtown.

Exit north onto 500 South Street, turn right, and head east across 700 East Street, passing Richins Office Design on your left (479 South 700 East) and Trolley Corners on your right. The Gothic Revival Richins building is a 1905 expansion of an 1886 adobe Congregational church. Trolley Corners is a deceptively new 1970s industrial-style building, designed to be compatible with Trolley Square. It houses 3 movie theaters and 2 restaurants.

Continue east one block to 800 East Street.

☛ Side Trip. One-half block to the north is Gilgal Park (452 South 800 East Street), behind an unnumbered private residence with a wood sign above the entry that reads "Fetzer." This park contains an unusual collection of religiously-inspired, Mormon-oriented statuary, including a sphynx with Mormon-founder Joseph Smith's head. The park is open to the public on Sundays. Knock on the door to let the owners know you are there. End Side Trip.

Turn right on 800 East Street and proceed south four blocks to 900 South Street. The houses in this neighborhood are predominantly 1920s Victorian cottages, California Craftsman bungalows, with an occasional stuccoed pioneer vernacular house that has survived the ravages of time. Just before the corner of 900 South

157

TROLLEY SQUARE AND LIBERTY PARK

Street, to your left at 847 South, is the 1911 Mountain States Telephone and Telegraph building.

At 900 South Street, turn left and ride east one block to the old Lefler Flour Mill on your left.

2. Lefler Flour Mill (859 East 900 South Street)

John Lefler established a successful mill here in 1879, powered by steam engine, supplying flour to local bakeries and restaurants. He was the last miller to operate the Chase Mill four blocks west until its closing in 1878. The mill later became known as Utah Roller Mills.

The building is a 2-story, stuccoed-brick structure, fronted by a 1911 addition in exposed-brick with a stamped-metal cornice. Notice the projecting balcony supported by ornamental brackets. The mill now houses Einstein Bros. Bagels and Gypsy Moon Emporium. This part of town includes a number of bohemian shops (notice the art-film Tower Theater across the street) some find reminiscent of Haight Street in San Francisco.

Cross 900 East Street and continue east up the hill two full blocks to 1100 East Street.

Cross 1100 East Street southeast onto Gilmer Drive. Follow it one-half block to the intersection with Alpine Place (930 South). Turn right and follow the winding Gilmer Drive past 1200 East Street, Michigan Avenue (990 South), and Herbert Avenue (1030 South) to Yale Avenue (1080 South).

3. Ivy League Neighborhood

This section of town is appropriately known as the Ivy League district. Not only are the streets named after prestigious universities, this is also where many of the University of Utah faculty live. An area of mature landscaping, period lamps, and undulating streets, notice the different periods of history and architectural variations. There is a predominance of 2-story Classical Revival homes, interspersed with Elizabethan and Tudor Revival designs with their steep, sloping roofs and half-timbering, and an occasional French-Norman or Chateauesque mansion.

You may want to take a fairly arduous side trip through the Ivy League streets to get a better look at the variety of architecture and landscaping. If not, turn right onto Yale Avenue and proceed west to 1100 East Street. You will pass the LDS Garden Park chapel on your left, built in 1939 on the 2.5-acre John Howard estate. The chapel replaced Howard's Italianate mansion, retaining the carriage house, pagoda, pond with balustraded porch, pedestrian bridge, and decorative brick wall along the southern property edge. There are walkways on either side of the chapel to the rear lanai. Howard was president of Utah Oil Refining Company. West of the chapel is a Boy Scout cottage designed by the chapel's architect Taylor Woolley, who was a protégé of Frank Lloyd Wright.

☛ **Side Trip.** Turn left on to Yale Avenue and ride east two blocks up the steep hill past Douglas Street (1240 East) to 1300 East Street.

Turn right and carefully ride south past the first Harvard Avenue sign (1120 South) to the second Harvard Avenue sign (1175 South) across the street to your left, posted above a one-way sign.

Turn left and proceed east on Harvard Avenue two blocks, passing Normandie Circle (1350 East), to 1500 East Street.

Turn right on 1500 East Street, proceeding south one block to Princeton Avenue (1165 South).

Should you want to take a break, just 3.5 blocks further south on 1500 East Street, clustered around The King's English bookstore, are Fresco's Italian Cafe, Einstein Bros. Bagels, and other shops. Return to this corner.

Head west on Princeton Avenue two full blocks to 1300 East Street, veering to the left at the intersection with 1400 East Street and then to the right at the intersection with Laird Avenue (1215 South).

At 1300 East Street, turn right and ride north one block to the second Harvard Avenue sign (1120 South).

Turn left onto Harvard Avenue and ride west two blocks to 1100 East Street, passing the LDS Garden Park chapel on your right. **End Side Trip.**

At 1100 East Street, turn left. Head south to Princeton Avenue (1150 South).

Turn right, riding west on Princeton Avenue past Inglewood mini-park (1040 East) on your left, crossing McClelland Street, to 900 East Street. At the corner of 900 East Street notice, across the street to your right (1144 South), the Saints Peter and Paul Orthodox Christian Church and private school, erected in 1902 as the LDS 31st Ward chapel. Notice how the architect, Joseph Don Carlos Young, blended Gothic Revival and Romanesque styles.

Turn left onto 900 East Street, traveling south—being careful to watch for traffic—to 1300 South Street where there is a convenience store and other shops.

Turn right at 1300 South Street, proceeding west to 700 East Street, again paying attention to traffic.

Cross 700 East Street and continue two blocks west to 500 East Street, taking advantage of the road/parking area that skirts the south edge of Liberty Park.

At 500 East Street, turn left, traveling south seven half-blocks, past Bryan Avenue (1560 South), to the Woodruff farmhouse on your right. There is an LDS chapel directly opposite (east) the farmhouse.

4. Woodruff Farmhouse (1604 South 500 East Street)

The Wilford Woodruff family compound began in 1860 as a two-room log cabin, which expanded as more children were born to become this 2-story stuccoed structure with a rear saltbox extension. It was built for one of Woodruff's plural wives. Woodruff, a Mormon apostle and later church president, served as president of the Utah Horticultural Society and the Deseret Agricultural and Manufacturing Society. It was here that he planted and experimented with a variety of crops. National Register of Historic Places.

Two houses south is another Woodruff house, his 2.5-story "villa."

5. Woodruff Villa (1622 South 500 East Street)

More than thirty years later in 1891, one year after announcing the prohibitive "polygamy manifesto," church president Woodruff constructed this neighboring domicile. With a carved stone bearing his name on the façade, this Victorian Queen Anne with an expansive porch and yard represented the ideal of the "Christian Home" movement, heralding the church's move away from polygamy and adoption of national norms. National Register of Historic Places.

Next door (south) is the Woodruff house.

6. Woodruff House (1636 South 500 East Street)

This Box Style house was built in 1907 by one of Woodruff's sons, Asahel Hart Woodruff, and reflects the continuing assimilation of national trends. The noteworthy porch features dainty Ionic-style capitals, dual columns, and fine wood dentil molding at the cornice. National Register of Historic Places.

Turn left at 1700 South Street and ride east one full block, passing Park Street (545 East), to 600 East Street where there is an elementary school on the northeast corner.

At 600 East Street, turn left. Proceed north to 1300 South Street. Park Cafe (604 East) is on the southeast corner.

Cross 1300 South Street and proceed north through the city's 60-acre premier urban park along the walk west of the artificial lake.

7. Liberty Park (600 East 1300 South Street)

To your left is the 11-acre Tracy Aviary (open daily 9:00 a.m.-6:00 p.m., adults $1.50, children $.75). Following the aviary, on your left, is the nucleus of the park, the "Old Chase Mill," in which Brigham Young was a partner. It was built in 1852 as part of what might be called Utah's first industrial park, a complex of eight mills and support structures. The flour mill was constructed of adobe and lime mortar. It is the oldest pioneer mill remaining in the city. Not open to the public. National Register of Historic Places.

Continue north past the Children's Garden playground (with ferris wheel), Park Patio cafe, arboretum and date garden (replanted daily to reflect the day and month) all on your left, and the Seven Canyons fountain on your right portraying the canyons which surround the valley. Following the fountain, on your left is the Isaac Chase home, built in 1854, which houses the Museum of Utah Folk Art. The original baking ovens in the basement are especially interesting (open daily in summer, weekends in spring and fall, 12:00 m.- 5:00 p.m. Closed winter).

Continue north out of the park. Cross 900 South Street and continue north on 600 East Street three blocks to Trolley Square where you began. This ends the Trolley Square and Liberty Park tour.

Liberty Park (VI.7)

VII.
Sugar House

DISTANCE: 8 MILES   TIME: 2 HOURS

1. Sugar House Park (1300 East 2100 South Street)

Begin at the 130-acre park which was the site of Utah's territorial prison, since demolished. It was here that about 1,000 Mormons were jailed beginning in 1885 for "unlawful cohabitation" (polygamy). The park entrances are on 2100 South Street at 1400 East, 1500 East, and 1600 East.

Take a trip around the small lake and fountains. You will be treated to a spectacular view of the Wasatch mountain range, including the Mill Creek and Olympus Cove neighborhoods snuggled at the base of the mountains. You will also pass behind Highland High School, followed by the Municipal Rose Garden.

Exit the park by way of the middle entrance at 1500 East Street (between a service station and fast food restaurant). Head north four full blocks to 1700 South Street, passing the former Garfield elementary school (now a day-care center) and a muraled LDS chapel—both on your left (west). The houses in this neighborhood include 1-story Victorian cottages, bungalows, and a few larger Victorian Eclectic homes.

Turn left at 1700 South Street and proceed west two blocks to 1300 East Street.

Cross 1300 East Street and continue west one-half block along the north edge of Westminster College, a Presbyterian school founded in 1875. Turn left into the parking lot and proceed south.

2. Westminster College (1840 South 1300 East Street)

Riding south through the parking lot, you will pass the Jewett Center for the Performing Arts and Payne Gymnasium (with small stone lions at the entrance), both on the right. Following these buildings, on your left with the prominent clock tower, is Converse Hall (now Jewett Center for the Arts and Humanities). This is a grand Jacobethan Style structure that dates from 1906 and was recently renovated. The rest of campus is equally impressive, and you may want to stroll across the grounds. The intimate, modern Nunemaker Chapel, reached by crossing a footbridge across Emigration Creek, is especially appealing.

After seeing the campus, circle back to 1700 South Street, turn left, and proceed about three blocks farther west through a small commercial center, passing a neighborhood park on your left (south), almost to the corner of 900 East Street. On your left is the 2.5-story brick and frame Cummings house with lavender and turquoise trim, since converted into a bed and breakfast.

Westminster College (VII.2)

SUGAR HOUSE

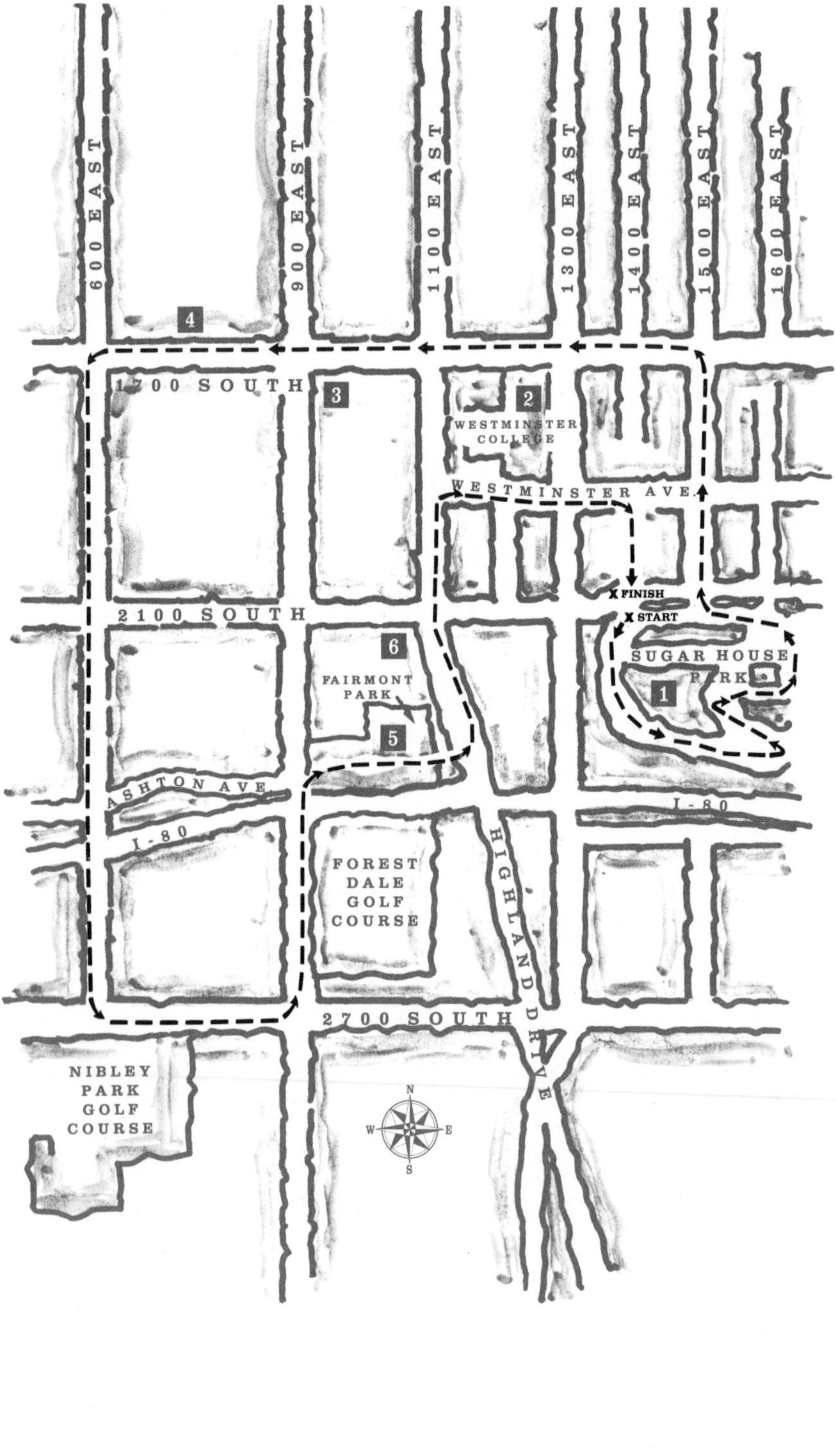

600 EAST
900 EAST
1100 EAST
1300 EAST
1400 EAST
1500 EAST
1600 EAST

4

1700 SOUTH

3

2

WESTMINSTER
COLLEGE

WESTMINSTER AVE.

FINISH
START

2100 SOUTH

SUGAR HOUSE
PARK

6

1

FAIRMONT
PARK

5

ASHTON AVE.

I-80

I-80

FOREST
DALE
GOLF
COURSE

HIGHLAND DRIVE

2700 SOUTH

NIBLEY
PARK
GOLF
COURSE

N
W E
S

3. Cummings House (936 East 1700 South Street)

Byron Cummings, a University of Utah administrator, purchased this Victorian Eclectic house in 1891. It was built as part of a pricey subdivision which developed around a trolley stop. Notice the ornate, arched window transom and the picturesque 2-story porch with ginger-bread trim. Cummings's neighbors included prominent saloon owner Henry Luce. This house is currently occupied by a bed and breakfast. National Register of Historic Places.

Cross 900 East Street and continue 1.5 blocks farther west, passing a grocery store on your right, to the Gothic Revival Arbuckle house, unnumbered but easy to find.

4. Arbuckle House (747 East 1700 South Street)

This well preserved 1.5-story brick house was built by George Arbuckle in the 1890s. Besides the steep-pitched gables and Gothic windows, notice the Gothic detailing on the porch and the upstairs doors leading to decorative, nonfunctional balconies. The most curious architectural feature is the fact that the window on the upper west wall is divided down the center on the interior by a wall separating a small bedroom and bathroom. Nineteenth-century homes rarely included indoor toilets, which were added as an afterthought. National Register of Historic Places.

Continue west another 1.5 blocks, passing an elementary school on your right.

At 600 East Street turn left (south) and ride ten full blocks, passing under a viaduct, to 2700 South Street. This is a typical inner city neighborhood with modest, well-maintained homes dating from post-World War I through post-World War II. Notice the similarity in design of the two Neo-Classical LDS chapels you pass, one on the left and another on the right, both built in 1925.

At 2700 South Street, turn left, riding three blocks east—with Nibley Park Golf Course to your right—to 900 East Street.

At 900 East Street, turn left, riding north along the west side of Forest Dale Golf Course, passing under another viaduct, to Fairmont Park.

Turn right at the Fairmont Park sign and ride east through the park.

5. Fairmont Park (2361 South 900 East Street)

This popular park was originally ten acres larger. When the freeway was built in 1962, the community rallied together to protect and revitalize this inner-city sanctuary.

Continue east to exit between the stone markers at the southeast edge of the park. Proceed east one block on Ashton Avenue (2310 South, unmarked), with a bowling alley to your left (north) and a state liquor store to your right, to Highland Drive (1160 East).

Turn left, heading north on Highland Drive through the Sugar House commercial center, watching for traffic. This shopping district dates from the 1930s and carries an air of nostalgia.

On your right, just past the post office, you will see the charming, Jacobethan Style Sprague Branch of the city library (2131 South Highland Drive), built in 1928.

Continue north to 2100 South Street. At this intersection, Highland Drive becomes 1100 East Street. To your left (west) is the Sugar House monument.

6. Sugar House Monument (2100 South Highland Drive)

This obelisk commemorates the indomitable spirit of the original settlers. Under Brigham Young's direction, they established a sugar beet factory here in 1853 with machinery imported from Liverpool, England. Although this ambitious venture was doomed to failure, they worked tirelessly for six years before realizing that they would not be able to successfully refine beet juice. The heroic bronze figures were sculpted by Millard Fillmore Malin in 1930 and the monument dedicated in 1934.

Cross 2100 South Street and continue 2.5 blocks north (with caution) along 1100 East Street to Westminster Avenue (1880 South).

Turn right at Westminster Avenue and ride east three steep blocks to 1400 East Street. Westminster Avenue jogs to the right slightly at 1200 East Street. Be careful crossing busy 1300 East Street. This neighborhood includes a number of elegant period revival cottages and small Bungalows.

At 1400 East Street, turn right, heading south. You will soon be back to Sugar House Park. This ends the Sugar House tour.

VIII.
Jordan River Parkway and Trail

DISTANCE: 11 MILES   TIME: 2.5 HOURS

1. Constitution Park and Northwest Multi-Purpose Center (1300 West 300 North Street)

Begin on the south side of the Northwest Multi-Purpose Center and head west on the sidewalk through the park. Turn right (north) onto the asphalt walking and bicycling path. Although you will be riding on asphalt most of this tour, there is a short stretch of unpaved trail.

2. Jordan River Parkway and Trail

Follow the east side of the Jordan River north. At the second bridge, after the trail curves to the west, cross the river into the park surrounding the Utah Department of Health and Utah Department of Agriculture buildings. Turn right after the bridge and continue north along the west side of the river.

Cross 500 North Street and continue north on the paved path, crossing the next bridge to the east side of the river and passing an elementary school on your right.

Cross 600 North Street and continue north along the trail on the east side of the river, passing the Riverside Park baseball diamonds on your right. The trail becomes dirt at 1000 North Street. (If you do not have wide-edged tires with liners, you may want to avoid this stretch of off-road terrain. If so, head west on 600 North Street to Redwood Road, turn right, and ride north to 1850 North Street.)

3. Rose Park Golf Course (1385 North Redwood Road)

Cross 1000 North Street and continue north on the east side of the river, with the fairway across the river to your left. Where the golf course spills over to the east side of the river, turn left to cross the bridge and ride west through the parking lot to Redwood Road (1700 West). Folklore has it that this road was named after the red stakes placed along this stretch to indicate to Colonel Albert Johnston's army of occupation, following the Utah War, how to reach the camp location decided upon in the truce negotiations. If you would like to take a short detour, there is a convenience store one-half block south on Redwood Road.

Turn right onto Redwood Road and ride about five blocks north to 1850 North Street.

At 1850 North Street, turn right (east) and follow the street zig-zagging south and east through the petroleum district and Water Reclamation Plant. At the east side of the reclamation plant, follow the road as it curves south. This is 1200 West Street (unmarked).

Follow 1200 West Street as it jogs east, continuing south past the

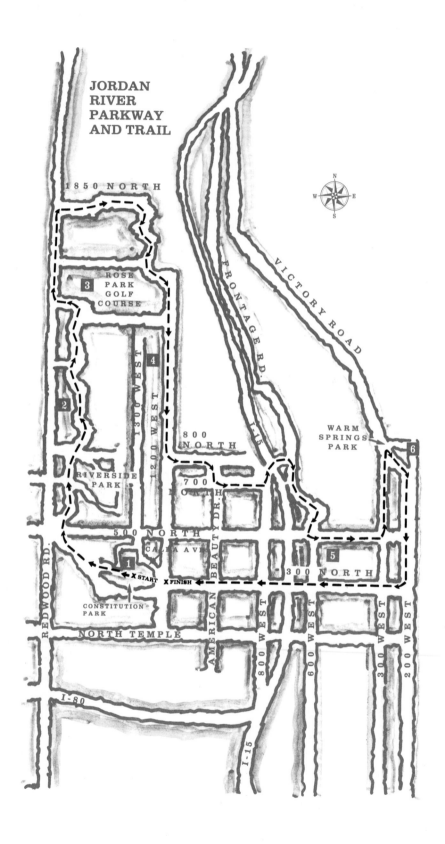

JORDAN
RIVER
PARKWAY
AND TRAIL

1850 NORTH

ROSE
PARK
GOLF
COURSE

3

2

4

1300 WEST

1200 WEST

800
NORTH

700
NORTH

RIVERSIDE
PARK

500 NORTH

CALLA AVE

1

X START   X FINISH

CONSTITUTION
PARK

NORTH TEMPLE

REDWOOD RD.

I-80

I-15

FRONTAGE RD.

VICTORY ROAD

WARM
SPRINGS
PARK

6

5

300 NORTH

BEAUTY DR.

AMERICAN

800 WEST

600 WEST

300 WEST

200 WEST

N
W   E
S

clay tennis courts and baseball diamond to your left (east) into the residential area. Continue six blocks south to 800 North Street, passing an LDS chapel on your right and the Rose Park Branch of the city library and an elementary school on your left.

4. Rose Park Neighborhood

This working-class neighborhood dates from post-World War II. Many of the homes were funded by loans sponsored by the Veterans Administration and Federal Housing Authority and built as suburban developments.

At 800 North Street (there is an LDS chapel on the southeast corner), turn left, heading east two full blocks to American Beauty Drive (1000 West), passing Steenblik Park on your left (north).

Turn right at American Beauty Drive, heading south—curving slightly—to Signora Drive (700 North).

Turn left onto Signora Drive, heading east (taking care in crossing 900 West Street) to 800 West Street.

At 800 West Street, turn left (north) and follow the curve east over the freeway overpass, biking (or walking) along the pedestrian sidewalk.

At the end of the freeway bridge, turn right to head south on the frontage road (700 West), following it around under the viaduct, passing the General Distributing Company (Anheuser Busch) warehouse, to where the street becomes 600 West.

5. Guadalupe Neighborhood

Many of the homes in this area are nineteenth-century, at least one dating from 1854. Before train tracks and freeway separated the neighborhood from the rest of the city, it was a fashionable suburb.

Follow 600 West Street further south to 500 North Street. The Guadalupe mini-park is on the southwest corner.

Turn left, heading east three blocks on 500 North Street, crossing the train tracks (and Pugsley mini-park on your right) to 300 West Street. (If a train blocks your progress, you may want to detour one or two blocks south on 500 West Street and then return to this intersection on the opposite side of the tracks.)

At 300 West Street (there is a convenience store on the northwest corner), turn left, riding three blocks north to Wall Street (800 North), which used to be the northern limit of the city. Be careful of traffic along this stretch. This U.S. highway (89) is still used as a truck route and commuter road to the suburbs north of Salt Lake City.

6. Warm Springs Park (300 West and Wall Street)

The mineral springs have been long-since dammed, but the 1920s Spanish Colonial Revival Style Children's Museum building north of the park used to be a public bathhouse. It replaced earlier versions, the first of which was built in 1849. Before the advent of indoor plumbing, people made weekly pilgrimages here.

Turn right (east) on Wall Street, following the curve southeast past Reed Avenue (750 North), to where the street becomes 200 West Street (Wall Street veering to the left).

Follow 200 West Street south, past the SandCastle Children's Center on your left (700 North), which is the former 24th Ward LDS Chapel, designed in the Queen Anne Style. Continue south past the E-Z Mart and Schmidt's Pastry Cottage (537 North) on your right and an elementary school on your left, to 300 North Street.

This is the Marmalade historic district, named after the fruit orchards which preceded most of the houses. The area is becoming gentrified as more of these pre-twentieth-century heirlooms are being renovated.

At 300 North Street, turn right and ride west ten blocks to 1200 West Street. You will pass (on the south side of the street) the Art Deco Style West High School, the Capitol West Boys and Girls Club and day care center, Our Lady of Guadalupe Catholic church, and the rear side of the Utah State Fairpark. At the end of 300 North Street you will arrive back at Constitution Park and Northwest Multi-Purpose Center where you began. This concludes the Jordan River Parkway and Trail tour.

IX.
International Peace Gardens

DISTANCE: 8.5 MILES   TIME: 2 HOURS

1. Doubletree Hotel (215 West South Temple Street)

In 1980 the Multi-Ethnic Redevelopment Corporation (now defunct) planned a hotel and cultural center for this block. A Holiday Inn was built in 1983, acquired by Doubletree Hotel three years later, and the rest of the development did not materialize. Since construction of a nearby sports arena, office buildings, and restaurant renovations, the hotel has become a popular spot to spend the night. There is parking across the street to the north at The Parking Place and next door to the west at the Diamond Parking Service lot.

From the Doubletree entrance, proceed east on South Temple Street a few yards to 200 West Street.

Turn right and proceed south, riding through the underpass, past the Salt Palace convention center to your left (east) and the 1-story Salt Lake Buddhist Temple on your right, to the Hills house.

2. Hills House (126 South 200 West Street)

This 1877 residence was built by Lewis Hills, one of the territory's leading financial advisors. It became the Hogar Hotel, a boarding house for Basques, and was since converted to The Antique Gallery. It is one of the city's finest Victorian Italianate houses. National Register of Historic Places.

Continue south, passing the 4-story Sweet's Quality Candies factory and 1-story Red Rock Brewing Company pub, both on your right; the 9-story Hilton Hotel to your left; and the 4-story Alpine Building to your right housing First Interstate Bank. Just past Bailey Place (755 South) is the intersection of 800 South Street with three large stop signs facing your direction. Studios for the local alternative radio station KRCL are on the northwest corner.

At 800 South Street, turn right, proceeding west. Ride through the traffic-light intersection at 300 West Street to the 3-story renovated brick warehouse on your right just before the railroad tracks.

3. Holt Seed Company Building (380 West 800 South Street)

Now housing architect, engineer, and real estate offices, this 1918 factory once processed and packaged grass seed and stock and poultry feed. The company was later called Occidental Seed Company in reference to its westside location.

Continue west, past Chuck and Marian's "Home-Style Cooking"

173

INTERNATIONAL PEACE GARDENS

Cafe on your left, across another set of railroad tracks. If a train blocks your progress, you may want to stop for a drink because it may be 10-15 minutes before the path is clear.

Continuing west, you will pass Mountain Cement company to your left, cross more railroad tracks, pass the Van Waters and Rogers chemical and synthetic textile warehouse to your right, and ride through an underpass.

To your right, after a railroad spur, is LDS Welfare Square. The tall, white grain elevators can hold 350,000 bushels of grain for disaster relief. In addition, the square warehouses and distributes canned goods, baked goods, and other supplies. A processing plant provides milk products for local Mormon, Salvation Army, and Catholic relief programs.

Continue another block west to 900 West Street. There is a convenience store on the northwest corner.

Turn left, heading south on 900 West Street across another set of railroad tracks to Jordan Park.

Ride past Montague Avenue (930 South) at the north edge of the park to the entrance just past the swimming pools. Turn right and ride west through the park to the International Peace Gardens entrance.

4. Jordan Park and International Peace Gardens (950 South 900 West Street)

This 21-acre park was established in 1918 when the city purchased the land for $25,000. The Peace Gardens were initiated in 1939 by the Salt Lake Council of Women and are now maintained by the Salt Lake City Parks and Recreation Department. They feature botanical displays representing flora and symbolic displays from twenty-four countries. Bicycles are not allowed, but you may want to lock your bike and take a peek inside. The Peace Gardens are open May-Oct., 8:00 a.m.-sundown; Oct.-Nov., 8:00 a.m.-4:30 p.m.

Proceed south from the entrance to the Peace Gardens through Jordan Park, with tennis courts to your right (west). Follow the eastern jog in the road to continue south between the baseball diamond on your right and LDS chapel on your left. You will emerge at Fremont Avenue (1100 South, unmarked).

5. Glendale Neighborhood

This working-class, ethnically-diverse neighborhood dates from the 1940s. The tract was developed by the Bowers Construction Company.

After exiting the park onto Fremont Avenue, turn right and ride west across the Jordan River to 1100 West Street.

At 1100 West Street, turn right, riding north around the curve that becomes Brooklyn Avenue (1055 South), continuing west one block to the T-intersection with Emery Street (1170 West).

Turn right onto Emery Street and head north 6.5 blocks to 400 South

Street. You will pass an elementary school on your left (west), cross railroad tracks, and pass Poplar Grove Park on your left. The farther you ride north, the older the houses are. One of the oldest is at 660 South Emery Street on the southwest corner of Arapahoe Avenue, built in 1923 by Joseph Tiano, a truck driver.

At 400 South Street, turn left. Ride west to Sherwood Park at 1400 West, passing La Frontera Cafe to your right (1236 West).

6. Sherwood Park (1400 West 400 South Street)

This area was known as Sherwood Forest when it was owned by Robert Sherwood, an LDS bishop. He donated the undeveloped property to the city in 1942.

Head north through the park (using caution at night) on the narrow sidewalk just past the Sherwood Park marquee, passing the playground to your left (west) and Little League baseball diamonds to your right, through the parking lot to 300 South Street (unmarked).

Turn right on 300 South Street and travel east one-half block past 1400 West Street to Navajo Street (1335 West). At Navajo Street, turn left, riding north through the underpass to 200 South Street.

At 200 South Street, turn right, riding east past a steel plant on your left (north), crossing the Jordan River, to the first house on the left after the bridge. The house is partially concealed by trees.

7. Fisher House (1206 West 200 South Street)

Albert Fisher, owner of Fisher Brewery, built this 12-room house in 1893 on the banks of the Jordan River to be near his brewery two blocks from here. The house was designed by state capitol architect Richard Kletting, mixing elements of Queen Anne, Romanesque, Eastlake, and Box styles. A rear, 2-story carriage house is also preserved. The house is owned by the Catholic church as a home for single males. National Register of Historic Places.

Continue east, past the natural gas company on your left, to 1000 West Street.

At 1000 West Street, turn left, heading north one-half block to Euclid Avenue on your right (140 South). Turn left for a brief tour of Euclid Avenue.

8. Euclid Avenue (140 South)

Notice the interesting and varied architecture, especially the newer, multi-dimensional, International Style homes at 1033 West and at 1014-16 West. Most of the development occurred in the 1910s. Residents were mostly blue-collar, including a railroad brakeman, a laundry washer, a delivery truck driver, and brewery workers.

Back at 1000 West Street, turn left, heading north across the railroad tracks, passing Madsen Park to your right (east), to North Temple Street. The buildings which house the annual state fair and occasional concerts are on the northwest corner, extending west, on a 64-acre campus. The oldest buildings date from the turn of the century and are on the National Register of Historic Places. A pedestrian entrance at this intersection is open during the fair.

9. Utah State Fairpark (155 North 1000 West Street)

The Spanish Colonial Revival Style Horticultural Building is the most visible structure from here. You may be able to see the Beaux Arts detailing, such as the colored arch over the doorway (including relief-stucco grapes, pineapples, peaches, and corn). This is the oldest structure at the fairpark and was designed by prominent Utah architects Walter Ware and Albert Treganza. Outside the Horticultural Building, facing the intersection, is a monument to the Donner Party which crossed by here in 1846 before being caught in snow in the Sierra Nevada mountains and turning to cannibalism.

Next door to the Horticultural Building to the west is the Grand Building, formerly the Mining and Manufacturing Building, in red brick and green-framed arched windows. The original entrance faced North Temple Street. It was designed by Walter Ware in Second Renaissance Style and completed in 1905. Outside the Grand Building to the north (not visible from here) is a Neo-Classical bandstand gazebo.

The grounds also include the 1913 Coliseum west of the gazebo (originally the Livestock Coliseum, a Neo-Classical building scheduled for restoration), a grandstand for viewing concerts, and rodeo grounds. Notice how the fairpark's buildings are unified by the warm color of the brick and similar trim colors. If you see any activity at the park, you may want to ride across the street and check it out. The entrance one block north is usually open. Return to this corner to continue the tour.

Head east along North Temple Street for four blocks, passing under the freeway, to 600 West Street.

Cross 600 West Street east to the road that runs along the south side of the overpass. Continue east one block. Just before the railroad tracks a ramp leads to a bicycle/pedestrian lane. Ascend the ramp and continue east. You will descend at an intersection with 400 West Street.

———

☛ Side Trip. At 400 West Street, carefully cross to the east, veering a bit to the north, to see City Creek flowing under North Temple Street below the chainlink enclosure under the viaduct.

From here you can also see the 5-story red-brick Salt Lake Hardware Store warehouse further north at 101-141 North 400 West Street. This 46,000-square-foot building with concrete lintels was the largest warehouse west of Chicago when it was built in 1909. It has 370 windows and 1,600 panes of glass. The company had wholesale outlets in seven states. Now the building is an investment of Gastronomy, Inc., restauranteurs.

Return to the North Temple Street pedestrian/bicycle off-ramp. **End Side Trip.**

Head south on 400 West Street one block to the traffic-light intersection with South Temple Street. To your right (west) is the Union Pacific Railroad depot in French Second Empire Style. Catercorner is the Delta Center where the Utah Jazz professional basketball team plays.

Proceed east on South Temple Street one block. To your left (north) in the foreground in red brick and green trim is the nineteenth-century Devereaux House, now the Chart House Restaurant, in front of the Triad Center office complex. These buildings are described toward the end of the Entertainment District walking tour.

Continue east one block to the Doubletree Hotel where you began. This concludes the International Peace Gardens tour.

X.
Red Butte Garden

DISTANCE: 7.5 MILES   TIME: 2 HOURS

To arrive at the Red Butte Garden and Arboretum parking lot where this tour begins, head east from the city by car on 400 South Street, which winds its way east becoming 500 South Street, to Wasatch Boulevard. At Wasatch Boulevard, turn left, proceeding north two blocks between the U.S. Army Reserve's Osborne Hall on your right (east) and the University Wasatch Clinics on your left to South Campus Drive. Turn right and proceed east through Fort Douglas on Hempstead Road to the stop sign. Veer a bit to the left through this intersection and continue east on Stover Street which winds slightly to the north. Exit the fort, keeping to your right, continuing east to the second parking lot on your right (south).

To arrive at Red Butte Garden by bicycle, proceed east from the city on 100 South Street to University Street (1340 East). Turn right, heading south, and proceed mid-tour at heading "4. University of Utah (western perimeter)" (below).

1. Red Butte Garden and Arboretum (mouth of Red Butte Canyon)

This beautiful public park consists of thirty acres of gardens, 200 acres of natural areas, and four miles of trails. Bicycles are not allowed, but you may want to lock your bike and take a stroll on foot. Late afternoon concerts are held here every other Sunday of each summer month. Admission is $3.00.

Immediately north of Red Butte Garden is an unmarked road that skirts the foothills and overlooks the university medical complex to the west. Proceed north on this road.

2. University of Utah Health Sciences Center (University Campus)

This sprawling campus includes the School of Medicine, College of Pharmacy, College of Nursing, two hospitals, research laboratories, clinics, state health facilities, and the Regional Dental Education Program. To your left are the twin Medical Plaza Towers housing medical students.

Continuing north through the parking lot, to your left (west) is the Biomedical Polymers Research Facility, followed by the Eccles Institute of Human Genetics, the Wintrobe Medical Research Building, the Dumke Biomedical Engineering Research Building, the University Hospital, and the Moran Eye Center.

Follow the curving road (North Campus Drive) down the hill out of the parking lot, through a stop sign, heading in a northwesterly

179

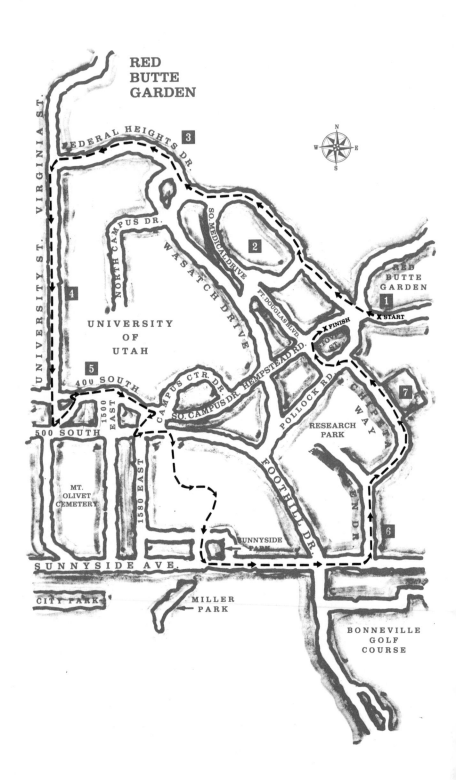

direction. Use caution along this stretch. The Fort Douglas Country Club is on your right (north), the Primary Children's Medical Center to your left. You will pass East Medical Drive on your left.

Turn right at your first available opportunity after the country club onto Federal Heights Drive (1695 East).

3. Federal Heights Neighborhood

At this upper elevation you can see the newest additions to the expensive homes of the Federal Heights neighborhood. Follow the curve around to the west, through three stop signs, to a T-intersection. This is Virginia Street (1250 East).

Turn left onto Virginia Street and proceed south to the second stop sign. This is South Temple Street, where Virginia Street becomes University Street.

Carefully cross South Temple Street, continuing south on University Street one block to the traffic light at 100 South Street. You will pass the Salt Lake Arts Council Art Barn Gallery and Reservoir Park on your right (west).

Cross 100 South Street, and continue three blocks south on University Street to 400 South Street.

4. University of Utah (western perimeter)

Riding south on University Street, you will skirt the western edge of the campus to your left (east). The first building to your left, facing 100 South Street, is the 1-story Ballet Studio. The next structure to your left, a 3-story building facing Presidents' Circle, is the old Student Union, now Gardner Hall serving the music department. On the opposite side of the horseshoe-shaped Presidents' Circle is an old campus library, now the Utah Museum of Natural History. The next building to your left, set back from the street, is Pioneer Memorial Theatre, followed by the College of Law and the old women's dormitory—Carlson Hall—now housing the history department.

Cross 400 South Street and continue south along the west side of the Rice Stadium parking lot.

Turn left mid-block into the parking lot and traverse the lot diagonally back toward 400 South Street to the northeast corner (toward the cement Social and Behavioral Science tower and yellow brick field house across the street in the distance).

Find the ramp leading to the pedestrian underpass. Ride north through the underpass.

5. University of Utah (southern perimeter)

On the far side of the underpass, turn right (east) and continue east through the railed/cement-walled alley along the south side of the field house.

Continue east through the parking lot. Cross the parking entrance roadway (1500 East) and follow the sidewalk east along South Campus

Drive (400 South), keeping on the north side of the street as it curves to the northeast. You will pass the Social Work building, Social and Behavioral Science tower, Museum of Fine Arts, Art and Architecture Center, Sculpture Building, and geyser fountain on your left.

At Campus Center Drive (1650 East), turn right and cross South Campus Drive to the south. Follow the curving sidewalk through the block to the intersection of 1580 East Street and 500 South Street.

Cross 500 South Street to the south and turn left, following the sidewalk east on the street side of the chain-link fence.

At the end of the chain-link fence—the entrance to Lot 1—turn right onto the road that fronts the Veterans Administration Medical Center parking lot. Follow this road as it curves southeast, with the hospital on your left and lighted baseball diamonds and tennis courts of Sunnyside Park on your right. You will emerge onto Sunnyside Avenue (840 South).

Cross Sunnyside Avenue to the south, turn left, and ride east to Foothill Boulevard. Although it is not steep, you may feel the effect of this steady incline.

Cross Foothill Drive to the east and continue riding east uphill. It is a little tricky here. Besides the fact that it is steep, the traffic is heavy.

Your first opportunity to turn left is Arapeen Drive. There is a traffic light here, a U.S. Post Office on the northeast corner of the intersection, and a University Research Park marquee.

6. University of Utah Research Park

This 150-acre campus used to be the military firing range. It was sold to the university in 1969 (part of which was donated to the state for This Is The Place State Park). The campus includes a hotel and university and private medical and earth science research laboratories.

If you would like to peddle further uphill to the historical park and zoological gardens, directions follow under the side trip heading.

——

☛ **Side Trip.** Continue east on Sunnyside Avenue one block to the entrance of This Is The Place State Park (2601 Sunnyside Avenue). This park includes Brigham Young's 1863 Forest Farmhouse; reconstructions of Mary Fielding Smith's adobe cabin and other pioneer houses; Old Deseret living history exhibits; sections of the Mormon pioneer trail; and This Is The Place Monument. The park is open 8:00 a.m. (spring, fall 9:00 a.m.)-5:00 p.m. (summer 8:00 p.m.) Entrance: $1.50 adults, $1 children.

Across the street to the south is Hogle Zoo (2600 Sunnyside Avenue). Open 9:00 a.m.-4:30 p.m. (summer 6:00 p.m.). Entrance $5 adults, $3 children. Be sure to see Gorgeous, the western lowland gorilla and his pet kitten, Njina, the bactrian (two-humped) camel, the orangutans, and the preserved "liger" on display in the Feline Building.

Head west on Sunnyside Avenue back to Arapeen Way. **End Side Trip.**

———

Proceed north on Arapeen Drive. You will pass the post office, Fire Station No. 10, and the U.S. Department of the Interior Bureau of Mines on your right (east). Midway through the western curve in the road is Chipeta Way.

Turn right (east) on Chipeta Way, following the curve around to the north. You will pass the University Neuropsychiatric Institute on your right. Just past Tabby Lane is the road which leads to the cemetery. Turn right to ride a few yards uphill to the cemetery entrance.

7. Fort Douglas Cemetery (Chipeta Way)

To your left (east) as you enter this 1862 military cemetery, interrupting a line of tall cottonwoods and locusts, is the original gate. At the southwest corner of the plat, the monument topped by an undraped male figure memorializes twenty-one German prisoners of war who died at Fort Douglas during World War I. The sculpture was created by Arno Steinicke in 1933. The most prominent people buried in the cemetery are camp founder Brigadier General Patrick Connor and territorial governor James Doty (1863-65).

Continue north on Chipeta Way across Wakara Way. The University Park Hotel is one-half block west on Wakara Way with a restaurant, gift shop, and restrooms. The hotel's Nicolodeon Bar is open 5:00 p.m.-midnight.

Continue north on Chipeta Way, past the large Northwest Pipeline Corporation building on your right. Cross the bridge to Pollock Road and turn left (west).

Take the next right onto Ft. Douglas Boulevard, riding north to the stop sign, which is Stover Street.

Turn right on Stover Street and proceed east out of the fort, further east one block to the Red Butte Garden parking lot where you began. This concludes the Red Butte Garden tour.

XI.
Upper Avenues and First South

DISTANCE: 7 MILES   TIME: 1.5 HOURS

To arrive at Memory Grove, head north on State Street to North Temple Street and turn right (east). Take the first available left turn (north) at Canyon Road, unmarked. There is a sign posted at this intersection, "Memory Grove Park— Closed to Motorized Vehicles."

Proceed north on Canyon Road for three blocks. If you are traveling by car, you can park right outside the grove.

1. Memory Grove Park (Third Avenue and North Canyon Road)

Proceed by bicycle north through the park. There are rest rooms and a drinking fountain at the north end of the grove to your left (west). A description of Memory Grove is given in the Capitol Hill and City Creek walking tour.

Continue north, riding through the car barricade, on the paved road out of Memory Grove to the mouth of City Creek Canyon. You can see City Creek flowing parallel to the road to your right. The climb here is steeper than it looks but soon gets easier. About one mile from Memory Grove, the winding road veers to the right just before it joins U-shaped Bonneville Boulevard. Follow the horseshoe turn across the bridge and through the car barricade onto Bonneville Boulevard. Proceed south in the bicycle/jogger lane to Eleventh Avenue. The climb here is easier than it looks. The hill on the opposite side of the canyon is known locally as "Gravity Hill" because cars appear to roll uphill.

———

☛ Side Trip. Instead of following Bonneville Boulevard south to Eleventh Avenue, you may head north into City Creek Canyon. At the point Canyon Road joins Bonneville Boulevard, turn left and then right (north) into City Creek Canyon. The paved road continues north about six miles and is open to bicycles on odd-numbered days. The canyon is open 8:00 a.m-10:00 p.m. Return to Bonneville Boulevard and proceed south on the east side of the canyon to Eleventh Avenue. End Side Trip.

———

At the top of Bonneville Boulevard turn left on Eleventh Avenue

(550 North) and proceed east along the marked bicycle path through two stop signs. There is a slight incline here, but you will pretty much coast through the rest of the tour after this. You are now in the Upper Avenues district.

2. Upper Avenues Neighborhood

Notice that the houses date from the 1950-60s and are predominantly Split-Level and Ranch Style, with a few structures that reflect period revival styles. You will pass the old Georgian Revival Style Veterans' Hospital on your left (north), built in the 1930s, and is currently being converted into condominiums. Take care crossing I Street.

Eleventh Avenue begins to wind after an elementary school playground on your left and the new Post Modern Style Fire Station No. 4 on your right. Follow the curving street further east along the north edge of Salt Lake Cemetery. You will pass the Spanish Colonial Revival Style Salt Lake Memorial Mausoleum on your left. At the next stop sign you will find yourself at Viginia Street (1250 East). Popperton Park is on the northeast corner. Shriners Hospital for Crippled Children is on the southeast corner.

Turn right at Virginia Street and head south, using caution as you descend. It is steep and easy to lose control.

Continue south to the traffic light, which is 100 South Street (First South). The Art Barn and Reservoir Park are to your right (west).

Turn right onto First South and head west 1.5 blocks to the brick house on your right (north) with the Flemish-gable façade.

3. Neuhausen House (1265 East 100 South Street)

Carl Neuhausen, architect of the Kearns mansion and Cathedral of the Madeleine, skillfully combined elements of old-world European architectural styles in this unique 2.5-story edifice which he built in 1901. Notice the unusual Flemish Baroque front gable and window trim, the lions' head reliefs on the columned portico, the rusticated foundation, and stone banding. The octagonal turret, tall chimney, and finials are Victorian Queen Anne influences. Also notice the leaded glass window transoms and domed dormers. National Register of Historic Places.

Continue west across 1200 East Street to the yellow, wood-frame house with white trim on the southwest corner (unnumbered).

4. Nelden House (1172 East 100 South Street)

Designed by Frederick Hale and built in 1894, this 2-story showpiece is one of the earliest and best examples of Georgian Revival architecture in Utah. Besides the rounded portico, notice the swan's neck pediments and finials capping the dormers, the dentiled molding, and other detailing.

William Nelden, the first owner, was president and owner of Nelden-Judson Drug Company. He committed suicide in early 1905. National Register of Historic Places.

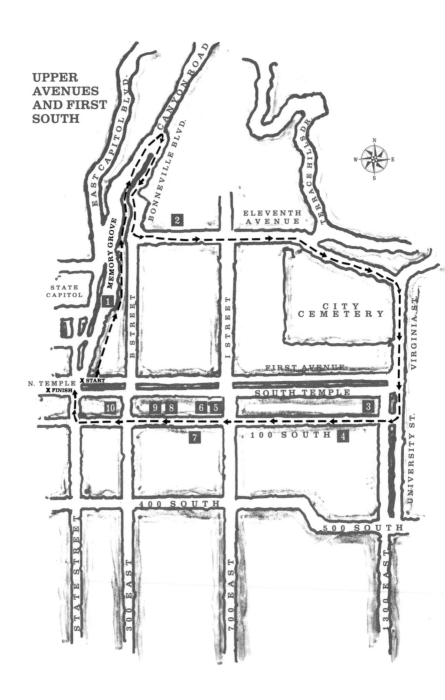

UPPER
AVENUES
AND FIRST
SOUTH

Continue west five blocks, passing the south wing of Holy Cross Hospital, an LDS chapel, a service station, and an intermediate school to your right. To your left will be Wasatch Touring bike and outdoor shop and several beautiful older homes.

Carefully cross 700 East Street westward to the Armstrong mansion on the northwest corner.

5. Armstrong Mansion (667 East 100 South Street)

Built in 1893, this stunning 2.5-story residence is one of the finest examples of Queen Anne Style architecture in the state. It was designed by William Ward, who carved the stone lion on Brigham Young's Lion House and helped design the Salt Lake Temple. He became disgruntled with Young's authoritarian rule and left Utah for thirty years. Notice the circular corner tower topped by a coned turret, stone banding, gable ornamentation, and fancy dormers. Francis Armstrong was a Salt Lake City mayor. National Register of Historic Places.

Continue west 1.5 blocks to the Bamberger house.

6. Bamberger House (623 East 100 South Street)

Built in the 1880s for Simon Bamberger, this 2.5-story house reflects the formality of Neo-Classicism with the playful detail of Victorian eclecticism. Bamberger was Utah governor from 1917 to 1921.

Continue west across 600 East Street. On the southwest corner is the imposing Salisbury mansion, now Evans and Early Mortuary.

7. Salisbury Mansion (574 East 100 South Street)

Designed by Frederick Hale and built in 1898, the Salisbury residence displays a heavy, rough-faced stone façade with 2-story, painted-metal columns, crowned by an enormous pediment. The crystal glass window transoms are distinctive. Orange Salisbury was a mining engineer and investment broker.

Continue west, passing the Eaton-Kenway tower to your right and the Boyer Company office building to your left.

Cross 500 East Street to the brick Hills house mid-block on your right.

8. Hills House (425 East 100 South Street)

This 2.5-story Queen Anne was built in 1905. An interesting touch is the Mission Style parapet on the dormer and the massive side porch topped by a decorative finial. Lewis Hills was president of Deseret National Bank.

Continue west two doors to the Dinwoodey house (unnumbered), now attorneys' offices.

9. Dinwoodey House (411 East 100 South Street)

Prominent Utah architect Richard Kletting designed this distinctive residence for furniture magnate Henry Dinwoodey in 1890. Subsequent occupants included Mormon leader James Moyle and U.S. senator William King. Notice, as with other houses on First South, the blending of renaissance and Queen Anne architectural elements. The ornate carved-stone porch entablature is particularly noteworthy.

Continue west for two blocks past the LDS church on your right and a convenience store and eclectic string of shops to your left. Utah's oldest permanent non-Mormon chapel is on your right just before the corner of 200 East Street.

10. Cathedral Church of St. Mark (231 East 100 South Street)

This stately, Gothic Revival cathedral, built of red sandstone from Red Butte Canyon, was completed in 1871. It was designed by renowned New York City architect Richard Upjohn, who designed Trinity Church in Manhattan and founded the American Institute of Architects. Although the eastern social hall is less ornate, together with the cathedral and northern addition, it creates an inviting courtyard fronted by the monastic-like arched walkway. Notice the rose windows in the gables, the narrow, Gothic nave windows, and the prominent belfry extending the height of the façade. Inside the cathedral, the 1857 pipe organ, built in Glasgow, Scotland, is the oldest in Utah. National Register of Historic Places.

Wells Fargo Company once had its stables and barns on this block, and later the coal-fired power plant which supplied electricity for city trolleys was located behind the church.

Continue west 1.5 blocks to State Street.

Turn right onto State Street and proceed north two blocks to North Temple Street.

At North Temple Street, turn right (east) onto Second Avenue, turning left at the first intersection onto Canyon Road, which takes you back to Memory Grove where you began. This concludes the Upper Avenues and First South tour.

Bibliography

Alexander, Thomas G. *Mormonism in Transition: A History of the Latter-day Saints, 1890-1930*. Urbana: University of Illinois Press, 1986.

_____. *Things in Heaven and Earth: The Life and Times of Wilford Woodruff, a Mormon Prophet*. Salt Lake City: Signature Books, 1991.

_____, and James B. Allen. *Mormons and Gentiles: A History of Salt Lake City*. Boulder: Pruett Publishing Company, 1984.

Anonymous. *Biographical Record of Salt Lake City and Vicinity*. Chicago: National Record Company, 1902.

Anonymous. "City Creek Historic District," in *Heritage* (27:3). Salt Lake City: Utah Heritage Foundation, May/June 1993.

Architects and Planners Alliance. "Survey Report for the Capitol Hill Historic District." 1976. Privately circulated.

Arrington, Leonard J. and Thomas G. Alexander. "The U.S. Army Overlooks Salt Lake Valley: Fort Douglas, 1862-1965," in *Utah Historical Quarterly* (33:4). Salt Lake City: Utah Historical Society, Fall 1965.

Brooks, Juanita. *On the Mormon Frontier: The Diary of Hosea Stout*. Salt Lake City: University of Utah Press, 1964.

Brunvand, Judith. "Frederic Albert Hale, Architect," in *Utah Historical Quarterly* (54:1). Salt Lake City: Utah Historical Society, 1986.

Campbell, Eugene E. *Establishing Zion: The Mormon Church in the American West, 1847-1869*. Salt Lake City: Signature Books, 1988.

Carr, Stephen L. and Robert W. Edwards. *Utah Ghost Rails*. Salt Lake City: Western Epics, 1989.

Carter, Thomas and Peter Goss. *Utah's Historic Architecture, 1847-1940: A Guide*. Salt Lake City: University of Utah Press, 1988.

Chamberlin, Ralph V. *The University of Utah: A History of Its First Hundred Years, 1850-1950*. Salt Lake City: University of Utah Press, 1960.

Esshom, Frank. *Pioneers and Prominent Men of Utah*. Salt Lake City: Utah Pioneers Book Publishing Company, 1913.

Foley, Mary Mix. *The American House*. New York City: Harper & Row, 1980.

Gillespie, L. Kay. *The Unforgiven: Utah's Executed Men*. Salt Lake City: Signature Books, 1991.

Goeldner, Paul. *Utah Catalog: Historic American Buildings Survey*. Salt Lake City: Utah Heritage Foundation, 1969.

Goss, Peter L. "The Architectural History of Utah," in *Utah Historical Quarterly* (43:3). Salt Lake City: Utah Historical Society, Summer 1975.

Haglund, Karl T., and Philip F. Notarianni. *The Avenues of Salt Lake City*. Salt Lake City: Utah State Historical Society, 1980.

Hilton, Hope A. *"Wild Bill" Hickman and the Mormon Frontier*. Salt Lake City: Signature Books, 1988.

Historic Preservation Research Office. "Structure/Site Information Forms." Utah State Historical Society, Salt Lake City.

Lakin, Dora L., and Marian B. Hopkins. *Historic Buildings Along South Temple Street*. Salt Lake City: Utah Heritage Foundation, 1980.

Lester, Margaret D. *Brigham Street*. Salt Lake City: Utah State Historical Society, 1979.

Lyman, Edward Leo. *Political Deliverance: The Mormon Quest for Utah Statehood*. Urbana: University of Illinois Press, 1986.

Malmquist, O. N. *The First 100 Years: A History of* The Salt Lake Tribune, *1871-1971*. Salt Lake City: Utah State Historical Society, 1971.

Malouf, Beatrice G., comp. *Pioneer Buildings of Early Utah*. Salt Lake City: Daughters of Utah Pioneers, 1991.

Mayor's Bicycle Advisory Committee. "Salt Lake City Bikeways Map." Salt Lake City: Salt Lake City Corporation, 1992.

McCormick, John S. *The Historic Buildings of Downtown Salt Lake City*. Salt Lake City: Utah State Historical Society, 1982.

Morgan, Dale L. *The State of Deseret*. Logan, Utah: Utah State University Press, 1987.

Papanikolas, Helen Z., ed. *The Peoples of Utah*. Salt Lake City: Utah State Historical Society, 1981.

Poll, Richard D., Thomas G. Alexander, Eugene E. Campbell, and David E. Miller. *Utah's History*. Provo, Utah: Brigham Young University Press, 1978.

Preservation Planning Office. "Utah Historic Sites Inventory." Utah Historical Society, Salt Lake City.

Raynor, Wallace Alan. *The Everlasting Spires: A Story of the Salt Lake Temple*. Salt Lake City: Deseret Book, 1965.

Ringholz, Raye Carleson. *Historic Buildings on Capitol Hill*. Salt Lake City: Utah Heritage Foundation, 1981.

Roberts, Allen D. "Religious Architecture of the LDS Church: Influence and Changes Since 1847," in *Utah Historical Quarterly* (vol. 43). Salt Lake City: Utah State Historical Society, Summer 1975.

Salt Lake City Planning Commission. "Salt Lake City Architectural Survey: Structure/Site Information Forms." Utah Historical Society, Salt Lake City.

Schindler, Harold. *Orrin Porter Rockwell: Man of God, Son of Thunder*. Salt Lake City: University of Utah Press, 1966.

Sutton, Wain, ed. *Utah—A Centennial History* (3 volumes). New York City: Lewis Historical Publishing Company, Inc., 1949.

Thatcher, Linda. "Lester F. Wire Invents the Traffic Light," in *Beehive History* (vol. 8). Salt Lake City: Utah State Historical Society, Sept. 1982.

United States Department of the Interior: Heritage Conservation and Recreation Service. "National Register of Historic Places Inventory—Nomination Forms." Utah State Historical Society, Salt Lake City.

Van Wagoner, Richard S. and Steven C. Walker. *A Book of Mormons*. Salt Lake City: Signature Books, 1982.

_____. *Mormon Polygamy: A History*. Salt Lake City: Signature Books, 1989.

Varley, James F. *Brigham and the Brigadier: General Patrick Connor and*

His Overland California Volunteers in Utah and Along the Overland Trail. Tucson: Westernlore Press, 1989.

Wadsworth, Nelson B. *Set in Stone, Fixed in Glass: The Great Mormon Temple and Its Photographers.* Salt Lake City: Signature Books, 1992.

Warrum, Noble. *Utah Since Statehood.* Chicago: S. J. Clarke Publishing Company, 1919.

Wells, Laura. "South Temple Tour." Privately circulated.

Whitney, Orson F. *History of Utah.* Salt Lake City: George Q. Cannon & Sons Publishers, 1892.

Glossary

ROOFS

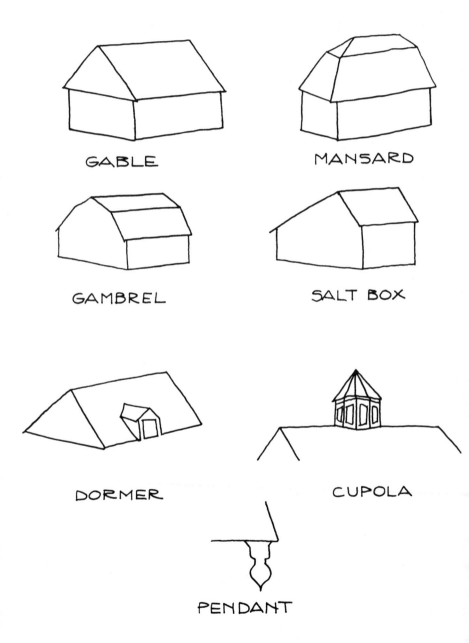

GABLE

MANSARD

GAMBREL

SALT BOX

DORMER

CUPOLA

PENDANT

WALLS

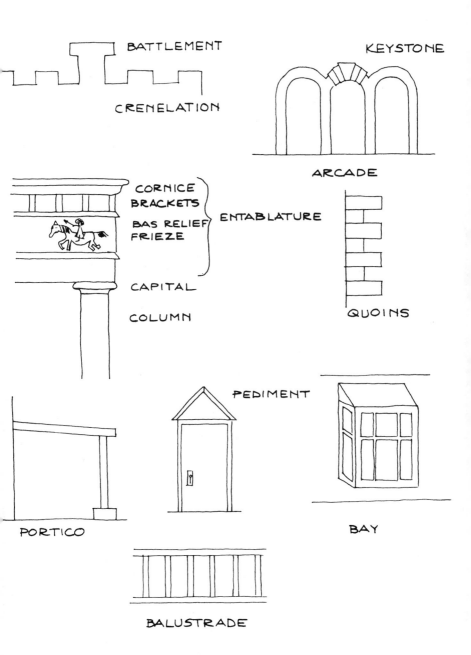

BATTLEMENT

CRENELATION

KEYSTONE

ARCADE

CORNICE
BRACKETS

BAS RELIEF
FRIEZE

ENTABLATURE

CAPITAL

COLUMN

QUOINS

PEDIMENT

PORTICO

BAY

BALUSTRADE

WINDOWS

LINTEL

TRANSOM

SILL

PALLADIAN

FANLIGHT

SASH

ROSETTE

CATHEDRAL INTERIOR

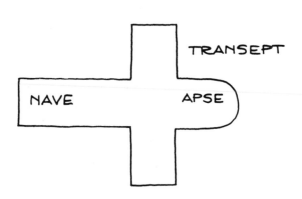

TRANSEPT

NAVE

APSE

Index